Spa Business
Secrets
To Increase Profits

The Best Published

Business Articles

To Elevate Your Success!

By Dori Soukup

Published by InSPAration Management, LLC
131 Executive Circle
Daytona Beach, Fl. 32114
www. InSPArationManagement.com

Edited by Jennifer-Crystal Johnson
www.JenniferCrystalJohnson.com

Library of Congress Control Number:

ISBN-10: 1495908267
ISBN-13: 978-1495908262

Printed in the United States of America.
Revised Edition 2019

IN⟨S⟩⟨P⟩⟨A⟩RATION

M A N A G E M E N T

For information on other InSPAration Management products, contact client relations at info@InSPArationManagement.com or visit:

www.InSPArationManagement.com

www.BecomePublished.com

www.DoriSoukup.com

Dedication

I dedicate this book to all the medi spa and spa entrepreneurs who shared with us their struggles, growing pains, and challenges, which led to us to creating effective business solutions for everyone to benefit from and elevate their success!

I dedicate this book to my son Charlie, who tolerated my travels while his father Craig took great care of him.

Maximizing Your Medi/Spa Profit Opportunities

If you are ready to maximize your business opportunities, this book is a must-read. It contains many great articles that were published in leading medi/spa industry magazines.

The topics vary from medi/spa management to team building, revenue streams, finances, and more... they will serve you as great bite-sized training to help you grow your business. Each chapter is filled with easy to implement systems, strategies, suggestions, and solutions to help you realize what you can do to maximize your opportunities.

Even though each chapter provides you with rich content, we decided to help you further by making additional recommendations of resources that are available for those of you who would like to learn more and take further steps to help grow your business. We also recommend that you register your book and receive several gifts that are included with your purchase.

Register your book and claim your GIFTS!
- Medi/Spa Capacity Calculator
- 5 Secrets to Profiting from Retail! An MP3 Audio
- A Complimentary Business Assessment and a Success Planning Session

Visit InSPArationManagement.com/free-spa-business-gifts to register!

Connect with us on Social Media!
To Your Success!
Dori Soukup

Table of Contents

Chapter 1:
Your Business Plan & Management Essentials

"Those who fail to plan are planning to fail!"
- Winston Churchill

How to Refresh Your Business Plan

In many cases, entrepreneurs usually create a business plan when they first decide to start a business and/or when they are applying for a loan. Once they achieve that goal and open their business, the business plan usually gets filed somewhere and rarely comes out for an update.

What about you? When was the last time you updated your business plan? Do you have the same vision and strategic plan you had when you first opened your business or has your business evolved without your business plan?

Time for a business plan check-up! Pull out your business plan and update the following seven strategies to ensure success.

1. Your Vision
All businesses are continually evolving and so should your vision. You may start with one vision, but after a few years, your business has probably changed. What is your vision for your business now? How clear is it? One of the most important parts of being a leader is to have a very clear vision and to share it with your team! When the vision is shared and understood, the team will help make it a reality.

2. Market Analysis
A business plan should always include a market analysis. Have you visited www.census.gov lately? You can gain all sorts of information regarding demographics and other statistics. Also, you may want to consider a focus group to gain knowledge about your target market or learn about their likes and dislikes, needs, and more.

3. Your Guest Experience and Medi/Spa Menu

For years the Medi/spa industry focused on pampering and indulging. But now, the focus should be on wellness and healthy aging. When was the last time you assessed your menu and made necessary changes to your guest menu and the experience? There are many wellness options you can participate in to help you tap into new revenue streams. If you desire to venture into wellness programs, you should get your hands on the "Journey Into Profits with Wellness Programs" audio. It will help you focus on wellness programs while increasing guest satisfaction and your revenue.

4. Marketing and Sales

I know people usually say, "sales and marketing," but the more accurate order is, "marketing and sales." You have to do marketing to gain sales. How effective are your marketing strategies? Have you looked into your Space Capacity Rate? If not, now is the time to plan for effective medi/spa marketing to drive traffic into your medi/spa. Then, make sure your team is ready to generate sales and increase revenue.

5. Financial Planning

It is vital to have a financially sound business. To do that, you need a medi/spa budget. If you have one, great! If you don't, you must. Visit InSPArationManagement.com and get a very easy to use template now.

6. Medi Spa and Spa Operations

Operations can be easily managed if you have systems, structure, and a plan. Every department should have its own manual to provide the team with operating guidelines to deliver a great medi/spa experience and do it profitably and consistently every time.

7. Team Building

Success cannot be achieved alone. Your plan should include a *dream team*! How effective is your team? Maybe it's time for a fresh start or to recruit some new team members. Hiring a highly productive team is essential in maximizing your business success.

Don't have a business plan? We do!

Whether you are starting a new business or want to refresh your current plan, you will benefit from this customizable medi/spa business plan. It will help guide you through all the necessary steps to build a solid foundation and provide you with a blueprint for success.

Dori Recommends….

To help you with your business, you can tap into the following effective tools:

- Customizable Business Plan
- Marketing Plan

Medi/Spa Management Essentials

Many medi/spa leaders and owners promote a person from their team to department lead or manager, thinking that because they are good at what they do, they will also be a good department lead or manager. The question is, "What management training are you providing to ensure success?" In most cases, the medi/spa does not offer structured management training for new managers or leads. This is a big void in most medi/spas. Is it in yours? **How skilled are your managers and leads?** Have they gone through management training? If not, read the following 11 medi/spa management essentials. It provides key training topics a new manager or lead should learn and master.

1. Defining the Manager's Role
You promoted someone to medi/spa manager or department lead. Now what? The first step is to define their role. What are their new responsibilities, how will you measure their efforts, and what are their goals? You must give a concise position description so there is clarity and understanding of responsibilities and performance expectations.

2. Establishing a Solid Medi/Spa Management Foundation
Now it's their turn to start managing. They need to establish a solid foundation. Create their department mission, vision, values, goals, and structure. They need to have a success plan and begin developing the team. If your medi/spa has department manuals, great! If not, you should have them as they are great training tools to help managers develop their teams and produce the results you seek.

3. Team Management & Communication
Management starts by getting to know the team and how to best communicate with each member. The new manager

must conduct a team SWOT analysis and discover who is on the team. Are they A, B, or C players? A manager is responsible for the team's performance. To ensure their success, the manager must know the ins and outs of how to help each team member excel. In addition, the manager must establish communication methods while realizing the importance of documenting events to keep the business safe and out of legal trouble.

4. Conducting Productive Team Meetings
Conducting productive team meetings is no small task. It takes preparation, planning the agenda, opening and closing strategies, clear message delivery, and motivation to positively influence the medi/spa team to take action. The new manager must discover the dos and don'ts of how to conduct a productive team meeting. If meetings are not well-planned, the manager will lose respect and trust. No one will want to attend future meetings.

5. Coaching the Team
Coaching is a big part of being a medi/spa manager and one of the most difficult things to learn. Becoming a great coach requires a lot of education, practice, skill, and experience. The coach must prepare for coaching sessions and be ready for obstacles that could potentially surface during the session. We teach the ICARE coaching model to help you build a high performance team.

6. Team Training
Training is everything! A manager must have a training curriculum for technical skills within the medi/spa business. This is missing from most medi/spas. In many medi/spas, training consists of having a product vendor conduct training about their products. Training must extend far beyond that. Becoming a great trainer takes skill, practice, and confidence.

7. Building a High Performance Medi/Spa Team

To build a high performance medi/spa team, a manager must learn how to recruit, interview, and hire the right people. Positioning new hires for success means doing a proper new hire orientation and training new hires how to succeed as a member of your team.

8. Managing Medi/Spa Team Communication

Medi/Spa managers are sometimes in a position where they must have difficult conversations with an employee. These types of conversations must be handled carefully with the right tone, message, and body language. Managing conflict and drama, dealing with negative attitudes, managing gossip, and reprimanding unacceptable behavior are not easy tasks. They all require training.

9. Motivating the Team

It's the manager's responsibility to ensure the team is focused, motivated, and producing positive results. The manager must know how to give constructive suggestions, offer empowering opportunities, and be a positive force. A great manager is one who provides frequent feedback while challenging the team to stretch, achieve, and excel.

10. Successful Medi/Spa Management Habits

Developing healthy business habits is a must for all managers. Some of those healthy habits should include conducting monthly performance reviews, coaching and mentoring the team, conducting positive meetings, while continually reaching or exceeding performance and guest satisfaction targets.

11. Understanding Medi/Spa Finances

To continue a manager's growth, it is important to teach finance. Whether you have a day spa, medi/spa, or resort spa, a manager should oversee the department's budget, minimize product cost and team compensation expenses, while tapping into new revenue streams to maximize capacity and profits.

Imagine having a manager who is educated and performs all 11 medi/spa management essentials! How much more successful would your medi/spa be?

Visit CoachMeOnDemand.com and discover Medi/Spa Management Essential tools to help you build your business!

SWOT Your Business

Everything needs a check-up every few months: our bodies, our houses, and yes, our businesses. Have you had a business check-up lately? If not, this is a perfect time to do it.

Start by doing a SWOT analysis for your entire medi/spa. What is a SWOT analysis? A SWOT analysis is an objective assessment of your current situation.

Take the time to identify your medi/spa's:

Strengths
Weaknesses
Opportunities
Threats

This will help you focus on your strengths, explore your opportunities, improve your challenges, and have a parachute to protect yourself. You can perform a SWOT analysis for every aspect of your business, from marketing efforts and sales to finances and operation.

One area many medi/spa entrepreneurs may not SWOT is their team. If you are medi/spa director or medi/spa owner, create a form with the SWOT acronym and ask each person on your team to SWOT themselves. Then, chart a path with your team to help you elevate your success!

Let's explore each letter of the acronym.

Strengths:
Every individual has strengths. It's a matter of identifying them and making sure that we build on them. When someone focuses on what they are good at, they feel great

about it and develop a passion for that particular strength. As a medi/spa leader, do you know each team member's strengths? Discover them and ensure that each team member plays the right role within your organization.

Weaknesses:
I prefer to call them challenges. What are your medi/spa's challenges? And what are your team's challenges? Is everyone aware of them and are there programs or an action plan to improve them? How long do you tolerate unaddressed challenges from a team member before you take action? What training programs do you have in place to help your team improve their performance? Training is a key factor and an investment that is worth making. Often I hear medi/spa leaders saying, "What if I invest in them and they leave?" My response to that is, "Imagine not training and them staying." Invest in training; it pays off big!

Opportunities:
There are many untapped opportunities within the medi/spa and the medi/spa team that go unnoticed. The question should be, "How can we increase guest satisfaction while increasing everyone's revenue and profits?"

This is a great team exercise. Schedule a brainstorming session and come up with new opportunities to improve your overall business. Some of those opportunities may include more treatment upgrades, more retail sales, more members, more series, and higher retention. The opportunities are endless! Outline yours and begin maximizing them.

Threats:
You need to be prepared for threats. Threats can be new competition, a declining economy, your health, or team

issues. Whatever they are, you must have your parachute ready. What is your back-up plan?

Conduct your SWOT and come up with an improvement plan.

"Welcome to Change Management 101.
We'll start with some free falls."

From OVERWHELMED to MISSION ACCOMPLISHED!

Planning = Freedom

Many entrepreneurs often feel overwhelmed. The list of things to do is probably a mile long and you often wonder, "Where do I start?" and, "When does it end?"

The first thing we need to identify is _why_ you feel overwhelmed. It's a fact... the number one reason people feel overwhelmed is due to:

1. Lack of planning
2. Distraction
3. Getting caught up in the Bionic Woman/Man Syndrome
4. Working IN your business rather than ON your business
5. Poor time management

To go from overwhelmed to mission accomplished, do the following:

1. Know what is most important to you
2. Put your success plan in WRITING
3. Integrate your success plan into your calendar
4. Stay focused on your plan

The goal is to go from feeling overwhelmed, confused, frustrated, and stressed to having clarity, organization, happiness, financial security, and most of all, peace of mind! Isn't this what most people want?

The first strategy is to identify what is most important to you.

Have you thought of this lately? What is most important to you? Is it making more money? Is it having more time? Or is it more freedom? What do you want? Let those reasons be the driving force to get you out of feeling overwhelmed. It's not enough to dream about it. Write it down. Make a prioritized list.

After determining your priorities, it is time to commit to change. Have you read the book *Who Moved My Cheese?* by Spencer Johnson, MD? Change is hard. But if you want different results, you need to do things differently… and that requires change!

The second strategy is to write out the plan.

Many people say, "I have my plan. It's in my head," or, "I know what I need to do." The important thing about having a plan is to share it with your team. You need to put it down on paper. Have you used mind mapping? It's a great method to outline your plan and identify the main aspects of each part. Yes, it will take time to write it out, but you will have clarity once you complete it. You will know exactly what you need to do and when. You will kiss that overwhelmed feeling goodbye! Just completing the plan will provide you with a great feeling of accomplishment.

The third strategy is to put Microsoft Outlook to good use.

Outlook is a great tool. If you are not using it, you should start now. It allows you to manage your time and block the necessary time to complete each task within your plan. Once it is on your calendar, you will block the time to complete the task in a timely manner. You will feel good about your accomplishments rather than feeling like there are not enough hours in the day.

The fourth strategy is to stay focused on the plan.

You've got to be consistent with your actions. Set your intentions and make the right choices. Don't allow distractions to steer you away from what you are trying to accomplish. Many people practice the "open door policy." My opinion is that, if you don't want to get anything accomplished, keep your door open. But if you want to work on your business, you better not only close your door, but *lock* it! It takes 21 days to turn a new action into a habit. You will feel uncomfortable at first, and that's ok. It's part of the necessary change process.

The fifth strategy is to know the value of your time.

Ask yourself, should I be doing this? Or can someone else do this task so I can work *on* my business? Is this task going to get me closer to accomplishing my goals? If not, don't do it. Know when to say NO!

There is a *major* difference between busy work and productive work. Productivity leads you away from feeling overwhelmed and toward feeling that your mission is accomplished!

Note: New results require new habits. Planning and productivity equals money in the bank!

Dori Recommends....

To help you with your business you can tap into the following effective tools:
- Visit CoachMeOnDemand.com for a wide range of tele-seminars that will help you.

Global Medi/Spa Business and Experiences

In the 80's and 90's, medi/spas were focused on pampering. Today, consumers are seeking and demanding health and wellness solutions as well. This is a noticeable global shift. Medi/Spas must make the shift or they will not survive.

The USA is the world leader in the total number of medi/spas. However, medi/spa popularity is growing around the world. Globally, people are interested in looking and feeling better, which helps maintain demand and ensures the medi/spa industry's growth. As a medi/spa consultant, I've had the pleasure of visiting 27 countries, speaking with many entrepreneurs and medi/spa leaders. In most cases, medi/spa business challenges are the same no matter where you are located.

The most common business challenges we encounter fall into the following categories:

1. Team Building - Employee Performance and Retention
2. Marketing - Operating the Medi/Spa at a Higher Capacity
3. Guest Experience - Guest Retention
4. Sales - Retail Sales
5. Operation - Systems, Structure, and Strategic Planning
6. Profit - Flat Bottom Lines

Global Medi/Spa Experiences and Business Practices

Most countries follow what we do in the US. They offer similar treatments for face, body, hands, and feet. The main differences are the countries' hospitality, customs, and conduct. Though many are promoting natural and holistic treatments, offering medical treatments plays a major role. Injectables, peels, and lasers are used in most of these countries. However, many don't have specific regulations and treatments may be conducted without a doctor.

In Seoul, South Korea, skin care centers are as popular as Starbucks is in the USA. Every corner has a beauty studio. Korean women love taking care of their skin. The bigger spas offer the typical treatments that are offered here, but most spas I visited in Seoul had large rooms with multiple treatments rather than private treatment rooms.

In Russia, it takes five years of schooling to be an esthetician. Education is very important to Russians aspiring to work as estheticians as they are basically doctors. That is why Russian estheticians in the US are in high demand. Russian spas use a wide range of beauty equipment. They also focus more on face over body. What was interesting is that most spas were connected to fitness centers, not resorts. Connecting resorts and spas is just now becoming popular in Russia.

The one country that surprised me the most with their lack of medical regulations is Canada. Currently, there are no regulations in Canada for most medical treatments. Anyone can perform laser and other medically related treatments. There are some associations, such as the Leading Spas of Canada, who are trying to establish a code of ethics to help protect the Canadian spa industry.

In Turkey, I had my most memorable experience with the Turkish Hammam. An experience like no other, the Hammam, which means "bathing" in Turkish, is a group experience. You lay on a slab of hot octagon-shaped marble and a therapist gives you a loofah scrub. Then they use soap and rinse you. You have never felt cleaner. It's customary to follow your Hammam with a massage. A fabulous experience! The Turkish Hammam is becoming more popular in the US.

Dubai has a similar feel to Las Vegas. Spas in Dubai are big and offer very similar treatments that we offer in the US. The main difference is that there are separate facilities for men and women. Sharing an experience is not a common practice.

My Malaysian spa experience was probably the best ever. The attention to detail and their protocols and rituals were executed with such perfection. Even though there was not much communication due to the lack of English, Asians pride themselves in delivering a great experience.

Plan your next trip and experience many of the great medi/spas around the world!

Hammam

Making a Family Business Work for You

The Challenges and Benefits of Working in the Family Business

I know a couple of things about family businesses because I grew up in one, worked in it, and know what works and what doesn't.

When studying the family business model, you have two main working groups:

1. Family members working in the business
2. Non-family member employees

This dynamic makes for an interesting work environment. Whether you fit in group one or group two, there are some golden rules to help you make the best of working in a family owned and operated business.

Family Member Golden Rules

Maintaining a Professional Environment
One of the biggest challenges in a family business is what I call the comfort zone. Family members are so comfortable with one another that communication becomes very casual, especially in front of non-family member employees.

Systems and Structure
This is often missing from small to medium-sized family businesses. Owners don't think they need systems, or if they have systems, they frequently don't follow their own systems or protocols.

Avoid Micro-Management

This is a big issue. Many business owners want to micro-manage. This practice causes processes to slow down because everything is dependent on one person making decisions.

Developing and Empowering Non-Family Members

Many business owners feel that if they invest in training and teaching their team new skills they will end up hurting the family business because, sooner or later, the person will leave and steal either their clients or their ideas. This is what I call "stinking thinking." Training is an essential part of building a business. If you don't train, you won't grow.

Refrain from Showing Favoritism

This is a biggie in family businesses and a big faux pas. Favoritism kills morale and motivation within the organization. Business owners need to recognize employees based on performance, not connections.

Non-family Member Employee Golden Rules

It takes a very special person to work in a family business, especially in a small to medium-sized business. There are many dynamics to juggle. If you find yourself working within a family business, keep in mind the following golden rules.

She Said, He Said Syndrome

You don't know who the leader is. He asked you to do one thing, she asked you to do another. You are caught in the middle of he said, she said, which is a terrible place to be. The most effective thing is for you to get clear and concise direction from one person and report to one person. This practice avoids drama and misunderstandings.

Position Description

Having clarity in your job responsibilities is a must. This doesn't mean you shouldn't go the extra mile or multitask when asked, but it does mean you clearly understand your role.

Blood is Thicker Than Water

Keep in mind, you are not family. Sometimes, you are put in a situation to take sides. It's best *not* to get involved. Do not talk badly about a family member. In the end, family members will kiss and make up, and you will be out!

Go With the Flow

Although it's good to be creative and make recommendations, sometimes we feel our way of doing things is better than their way; but keep in mind, it's not your business. You need to go with the flow and pick the battles you can win.

Professionalism

The best golden rule is to always maintain a professional relationship with all family members, non-family members, and other co-workers. Have a positive attitude, keep smiling, be helpful to others, and go beyond what is expected of you.

Working in a family business can be great! It's much more flexible than the corporate world. You'll find family businesses are more compassionate, understanding, and caring. If you are looking for a new career or you've never worked for a family business, maybe now is the time to try it, or maybe it's time for you to start your own family business!

Chapter 2:
Smart and Economical Marketing Strategies

"You can have brilliant ideas, but if you cannot get them across, your ideas will not get you anywhere."
- Lee Ioacocca

Marketing Plan, Your Number One Priority!

Do you have a marketing plan?

If not, you are not maximizing your true potential and you're probably not operating at your true capacity, either. Marketing is one of the most important functions of operating a medi/spa successfully. When your team is busy and your treatment rooms are full, it seems that all other problems go away. It's when your team is sitting around not doing anything that things go from bad to worse!

If you want to set new performance records, you must focus on marketing. There are different types of marketing methods: basic marketing and trust-based marketing.

Basic Marketing and Trust-Based Marketing

Basic Marketing is when you directly promote a product or service to a mass market segment. An example of basic marketing would be to run a Groupon or a Living Social deal designed to bring in deal-seekers (bad idea).

Trust-Based Marketing focuses on building relationships with a specific target by building trust and maintaining a long-lasting relationship.

Effective Trust-Based Marketing Options

- Create a newsletter
- Host events
- Offer wellness and beauty tips through social media
- Share testimonials and success stories
- Offer a loyalty and appreciation program
- Stay in touch and always under-promise and over-deliver

When you build trust with your clients and your team, you will be able to take your business to a whole new level. Remember, word of mouth is a powerful marketing tool! When you go beyond your competition and deliver exceptional guest experiences, you can take your company viral with great comments and reviews.

Seven Easy Steps to Help You Create Your Marketing Plan

Again, marketing is one of the most important keys to your success. Without marketing, you won't maximize your medi/spa's capacity or your revenue generation. You need to have an annual marketing plan in order to ensure a steady flow of new and repeat guests visiting your medi/spa. Having a marketing plan is what separates a successful business from one that is barely surviving. Here are seven easy steps to help you create your marketing plan.

1. Take some time to focus on your marketing needs.
Do a business assessment. Evaluate what is working and what needs to change. Then, plan your annual marketing efforts.

2. Identify your target market.
Who are your clients? Create a client profile that best describes your clients. Research their demographics (age, income, lifestyle) and psychographics (likes and dislikes).

3. Match the right menu and price to your target market.
Is your menu selling your services or is it just a price list? Does it describe treatments in enticing ways that make clients say, "I want that treatment?" Refresh your offerings focusing on wellness and beauty.

4. Set a marketing budget.
Many people think that marketing requires large budgets, but that is not the case. There are many economical

marketing strategies you can participate in. Practice this rule of thumb: invest 10% of your gross revenue into marketing. Determine your monthly marketing investment and apply it to your economical marketing mix to help increase exposure and traffic.

5. Choose your marketing mix.
Many medi/spa owners think that advertising is the main type of marketing to participate in, but that is not the case. There are many marketing mix options to choose from. In the Leap Ahead Medi/Spa Leaders Seminar, we cover over 57 different economical marketing strategies you can participate in and that are designed specifically to increase your traffic and revenue.

6. Develop your marketing material.
Your marketing material needs to match your image and deliver a compelling message to take action. Too often we see menus, brochures, ads, or email blasts that don't ask the target market to take action.

7. Plan your marketing calendar.
Here is the biggest mistake we encounter. Many people don't have a marketing calendar for the entire year! Without a calendar, you are reacting rather than planning. For example, in January you should be planning for Valentine's. It should be on your calendar with a list of things that need to be done in advance to insure a profitable Valentine's *month*. Yes, *month...* not just day.

Take time this month to assess your marketing needs and plan your entire year. Don't delay, start now! Take time to plan your success!

Need help with your marketing? We specialize in marketing!

Dori Recommends….

To help you with your business you can tap into the following effective tools:

CoachMe Gold

Genius Marketing and Sales Strategies. Listen to 24 hours of marketing strategies or read transcripts of each module.

A Marketing Plan

You can customize. All ready for implementation.

Register your book and receive 20 economical marketing strategies!

Building Your Medi/Spa List

During the Leap Ahead Medi/Spa Leaders Seminar I ask the attendees, "What is your list-building strategy and how do you generate leads?" Most of the time I get very basic answers with no solid strategy or plan for list-building.

Most medi/spa owners do the basics: they have a website, they may do events, maybe advertise, a little social media, a little of this and that. Many still operate under the old adage, "If you build it, they will come."

If your business is not growing, all you have to do is assess your lead generation efforts and see how many new guests you are obtaining per day, week, and month; this will be your indication of how well you are doing with lead generation and efforts to grow your business. Medi/spa business growth starts with lead generation, but that's only the beginning.

First you must know the answers to the following questions:
- How many new leads do you generate per month?
- What is your conversion rate from lead to guest?
- What is your average lead cost?
- What is your guest value per visit?
- What is the client lifetime value?
- What is your current retention rate?

Do you know the answers to these questions? If yes, congratulations! If not, you need to.

The second factor is to know the cycle to generating and building your list.
- Marketing efforts to attract leads.

- An offer to entice them to "opt in" to your email list.
- Initial communication.
- Offer to *convert* them into a guest.
- Wow them so they can become a lifetime client.

You are probably thinking, *ok, this makes sense but how do I do it?*

You can do it by tapping into the content on a USB program called *Build Your List and Grow Your Business* where I teach the BEFRIENDS System! The BEFRIENDS System is designed to make list-building easier and help you increase your revenue and profits. It provides you with a blueprint to help you build a spa list of your target market so you can market to them directly and grow your business.

BEFRIENDS is an acronym that stands for the following:
B. Building your list
E. Essential management tools
F. Finding your target market
R. Rewards for double opt-in
I. Identifying where to generate leads
E. Engaging through automated sequencing
N. New offer to convert leads into clients
D. Developing relationships
S. Sustainable growth

People often ask me, "What is the easiest way to build a list?" On the USB I share 16 ways to get people to opt-in to your list and over 25 ways to generate leads and turn them into guests and lifetime clients.

Here are a couple of examples of how to entice people to "opt-in" from your website and become part of your community!

- Create a report that will be of interest to your target market
- Give them the opportunity to download audio about how to stay healthy and beautiful
- A recipe for weight management

Placing a noticeable "Opt-In" on the home page is a must. If you don't have something to entice people to opt-in, you will never have the chance to get them on your list and you will not be able to begin a relationship with them that will lead them to become clients. When they opt-in is the time to begin communicating with them and work towards converting them into guests.

You must set up automated sequences to begin building a relationship!

Here are few examples of where to generate leads:

- Your website is one of the most economical places to generate leads
- Joint venture with another business is one the best and fastest ways to generate leads
- Direct mail. Use the U.S. postal service EDDM, Every Door Direct Mail. Focus on taking an offline marketing campaign and turning it into an online lead.

Another key component of growing your business is building relationships. That is why we called this system the BEFRIENDS System. When you build relationships, clients will stay with you longer and spend more money.

The best way to build relationships is by providing appreciated communication, benefits, value, respect, and trust. If your entire relationship is based on those values, you will have lasting relationships.

When working with new clients, I ask them, "Do you have a newsletter?" In most cases, I hear no. Having an e-zine is one of the best ways to build relationships and position yourself as an expert.

Visit InSPArationManagement.com/spa-biztools and choose from several products we have to help you!

1. Ready-To-Go E-zine
2. Done For Me Marketing

The e-zine plays a big role in lead generation. It has many benefits. Here are a few:

- Have other businesses send it out on your behalf so people can subscribe to it
- Send it out to a new lead who opts in to help position you as an expert
- Archive it on your website for better SEO positioning
- Inform your list of your promotions
- Add value and maintain an open line of communication between you and them

We invite you to opt in to InSPAration Moments, your e-zine partner. We have been publishing InSPAration Moments for over five years; it goes out every first of the month like clockwork. It has helped build great relationships and a profitable business. You can do the same! Go to the InSPAration Moments page on InSPArationManagement.com to view the current issue.

Dori Recommends....

To help you with your business you can tap into the following effective tools:

Six Medi/Spa Website Alerts

Here are six key questions to help you identify improvements to make your website more effective.

1. Is your website more than just an online brochure?

Many people make the mistake of simply creating a website that is nothing more than an online company brochure. If consumers happen to stumble on it, they may stay for less than a minute, then leave with no desire to ever come back. These types of sites kill your online efforts. They lack engagement and communication. All they talk about is "our this" and "our that."

2. Is your website engaging your visitors?

Many websites we visit don't give consumers the opportunity to begin building a relationship by engaging them as soon as they arrive on the home page. They lack rich content, conversation starters, and engagement.

3. Is your website helping to build your client list?

Rarely do I see a medi/spa website home page that captures people's information. This is a key tool that will help build your client list and expand your database. How many ways do you have on your home page to capture your visitors' information and build your list?

4. Is your website copy capturing visitors' attention?

Is your copy clear and focused on benefits? In most cases, medi/spa website content lacks a call to action or complimentary offers to entice your visitors to opt-in to your list. Are you sharing information that is important to your visitors? Are you helping them solve their problems and challenges?

5. Is your website generating revenue?

Large sums of revenue can be generated from your website, if marketed properly. Selling gift cards and products online is a great revenue source to increase your overall profits. Make the shopping experience super special and user-friendly.

6. Do you track and measure your website visits?

Google Analytics is a free service you can sign up for to see how much traffic you receive on your website and how long people are staying once they visit your page. Tracking your performance is the key to knowing why you need to make changes. Take the time to review how well your website is performing and make it better!

Use these six questions as a guide to develop your website. Answer the key questions to help you identify improvements so your website can be a more effective, revenue-generating tool. Visit InSPArationManagement.com and purchase the *Make Your Website Work For You* USB.

Loyalty and Client Retention

In the early 1980's, American Airlines' goal was to increase retention and provide their clients with something extra special. The airline created the first frequent flyer program that allowed travelers to accrue miles and gain benefits as long as they were flying with American. American Airlines was one of the first companies to offer a customer loyalty program in the country. It set the standards for the entire industry.

Since then, loyalty programs have gained significant popularity. According to a recent study, companies spend more than $2 billion on loyalty programs per year. Statistics show the average American household belongs to about 14 different rewards programs.

If you want to increase your retention rate, it's your turn to offer your clients a loyalty program that will keep them coming back.

What type of loyalty program should you offer?
There are several types of programs to offer consumers and, no matter which one you choose, it's important to keep it simple. Below are two of the most effective loyalty programs:

A. Charge a fee to join the loyalty program. For example, Barnes and Noble charges its clients $25.00 to join their loyalty program. Then, its members can save 10% on their purchase the entire year. For a person like me who frequents Barnes and Noble weekly, this type of program provides great benefits. The savings at the end of the year are significant. This program keeps me loyal to Barnes and Noble and it's worth it to pay the $25 to join. You can do the same, but I recommend you charge more. For example, you can charge $150 to join and offer them the following:

- Two $25 gift cards to be utilized one at a time
- A complimentary consultation valued at $50
- A complimentary makeover valued at $50
- A loyalty welcome kit
- 5% to 10% off of every medi/spa visit and/or retail purchase

You are giving them the $150 enrollment back in value. This allows you to raise cash flow and encourage the new member to visit the medi/spa on a regular basis. As part of the loyalty program, the client will benefit by receiving a small discount with each medi/spa visit.

B. The second plan allows clients to join free and earn points for every visit. You can reward them by crediting one point for every dollar they spend. Once they reach a certain amount of points, they can redeem their points with gifts, services, or products.

You will need to determine the amount of rewards you are willing to offer. For example, if someone spends $500, they will earn 500 points. If you wish to offer them a 10% reward you will need to select a $50 prize they can have once they reach 500 points. This represents a 10% reward. If you are offering this type of loyalty program, I recommend you offer merchandise as a reward because your cost will be $25 but the client will receive a value of $50. This practice allows you to decrease your loyalty cost to a 5% reward instead of 10%.

Select gift items that you can brand with your logo such as robes, t-shirts, hats, water bottles, etc. This method has many benefits:

1. Provides your loyal clients with desirable, quality gifts
2. Gifts are a great way to promote your business
3. Shows a higher perceived retail value while reducing your loyalty cost
4. Saves money and increases retention

The point system can also be used as a marketing tool. If you have some slow slots within your schedule, you can reward your clients with double points on slow days or hours. Instead of offering discounts, offer double points for promotions. You can ask your clients to write reviews to earn points or "like" your page to earn points, too.

Keep in mind that no matter which program you offer, you have to market it, track it, and deliver a great guest experience. Offering a loyalty program is a great opportunity to promote your business and increase retention rates.

Dori Recommends….

To help you with your business you can tap into the following effective tools:

Launch a Membership and Loyalty Program USB

Ten Gift Card Success Strategies

Gift cards are one of the most popular gift-giving options among consumers. Studies show that about 81% of American adults will purchase at least one gift card during the holiday season according to a Retail Federation survey. This makes gift cards one of the most popular Christmas presents of all.

From a business owner standpoint, studies indicate that a shopper using a gift card to make a purchase will likely spend 40% more than the value of the card. Also, 41% of gift card recipients will visit a new store because of a gift card and 72% of gift card recipients make a return trip to the store. (Source: *Shopatron, an ecommerce platform.*) This is great news for all medi/spas!

Within the medi/spa industry, gift card sales should represent a large portion of revenue. It's an easy revenue stream to maximize if it is positioned, marketed, and managed properly. However, most of the time we come across the following challenges:

1. Teams view gift card clients as unqualified clients. They don't believe that they are medi/spa goers; therefore, they pre-judge them and don't attempt to convert them into lifetime clients.
2. They don't attempt to upgrade them or recommend buying home care products.
3. The medi/spa owner uses the funds from gift card sales to manage their financials prior to gift card redemption.

4. The medi/spa attempts to sell gift cards mainly during special calendar months such as Valentine's Day, Mother's Day, and the holiday season instead of focusing on gift card sales throughout the entire year.

10 Gift Card Success Strategies

1. Gift Card Funds Management: Open a separate account for gift card sales. Gift card sales should only count as a sale when the guest redeems the card. This will help you avoid the practice of borrowing from Peter to pay Paul. Improper accounting can get out of hand very quickly and cause your business to be at financial risk.

2. Maximize Gift Card Revenue with Retail: Create gift card offers that include retail products. Maximize revenue by offering retail options with gift card sales. This will enhance gift giving as well as increase your retail sales and the size of each gift card transaction.

3. Online Gift Card Sales: Make a big splash about gift card giving on your website. This is often a missed opportunity. Place a gift card opportunity on each page of your website, not only the home page. Make it easy and enticing for consumers to purchase gift cards.

4. Team Generated Sales: Train the guest relations team how to promote gift cards. The last phrase your receptionists should say prior to completing the checkout process is, "Any birthdays, anniversaries, or special occasions for someone in your life who would love to have a medi/spa gift card?" This statement alone will remind many of your clients to take action and purchase a gift card now.

5. Performance Expectations and Rewards: Set performance targets and offer a reward program for your guest relations team to promote gift card sales. This will motivate them to ask and offer gift card suggestions, increasing your revenue.

6. Encourage People to Use Their Gift Cards: Don't think because someone did not use the gift card that it's a good thing. It is not. You are losing the opportunity to turn them into a repeat client. Also, if gift card holders do not redeem the card, you are hurting future sales due to the fact that the person who purchased the gift card for them will not purchase another one. Have a system in place to contact the gift card recipient to encourage them to make an appointment and turn them into a client.

7. Combine a Gift Card Offer with a Charitable Organization: Many medi/spas receive inquiries to donate to charitable organizations. Normally medi/spas donate a gift of some sort. Instead, give $10 gift cards to all attendees, include your menu, and invite them to visit your medi/spa. This will provide major exposure for your medi/spa and help you generate many new clients, leading to a lot more revenue.

8. Deliver a Great Guest Experience: Teach your team how to treat a first-time gift card user. Show them the potential of this new client and how they could help them earn more money. As mentioned above, gift card clients spend more *and* come back. A gift card client should be celebrated! It Is an opportunity for everyone to benefit from their visit.

9. Stay Legal: Know your state's laws regarding gift card expiration dates and gift certificates so you don't get into a legal mess.

10. Buyers Info: Currently, most medi/spas focus on receiving the info of the person who is receiving the gift card. That is the norm. However, if you take the time to obtain complete information for the person who is buying the card, too, such as name, email address, and phone number, you will be able to segment this person in your database and send specific marketing messages so they will buy your gift cards over and over again.

Your Medi/Spa's E-zine!

In speaking with members of our community, potential clients, and medi/spa professionals, I often ask if they have an e-zine. Frequently their response is no. It's also interesting to hear what some people consider an e-zine to be. For those of you who have one, have you assessed the effectiveness of your e-zine lately?

Your e-zine should:
1. Provide your clients with rich content to strengthen the relationship.
2. Grow your list to market to on a regular basis.
3. Effectively promote your services or products.
4. Position yourself as an expert in your field.

Your e-zine should have a similar structure to the InSPAration Moments e-zine.
a. Establish your positioning
b. Give your e-zine a name
c. Use structure – be consistent with your outline and main categories. Use them every month.

> **Suggested structure:**
> 1. A Note from the Leader
> 2. Featured Article
> 3. Medi/Spa Cuisine Recipe
> 4. Ask a Therapist, Doctor, or Nurse
> 5. Success Stories
> 6. Medi/Spa Recommendations
> 7. Promotions
> 8. Events or Happenings
> 9. Register to Win

Many people don't realize how important an e-zine is to a business. That's why they don't focus on it. Today, I want to highlight these important points so you can create or improve your e-zine. As mentioned earlier, there are four key reasons to have an e-zine. Let me expand on each one:

1. Provide Your Clients with Rich Content to Strengthen the Relationship

In many cases, rich content is missing. Many people think sending out email blasts is all you need to do. If all you are sending is, "buy from me," your audience will lose interest and typically hit "delete" before they even look at it. In fact, too many "buy from me" email blasts will get people to "opt out" from your list. *Rich content is very important!* Give your readers valuable information they can use! What rich content are you delivering?

2. Grow Your List to Market to on a Regular Basis

Many medi/spas don't have lead generation strategies. We emphasize the importance of building your list during the CoachMe Gold modules. Your e-zine can help you build your list, not only from your website but from B2B relations. With a great e-zine, this process becomes achievable; you will build a great list quickly that you can market to over and over.

3. Effectively Promote Your Services or Products

Through your e-zine, you can promote your products or your special offers. Again, this is just like what you see in InSPAration Moments. We provide value while promoting certain products to help you with your business. It's a win-win for everyone!

4. Position Yourself as an Expert in Your Field

By offering valuable information that is helpful to your readers, you become the expert. You own a medi/spa. It's about helping people feel and look their best! How are you helping them now? You can do a lot more through your e-zine. Share your knowledge!

Frankly, you can't afford not to have a newsletter. It's one of the most important marketing tools to have.

Dori Recommends….

To help you with your business you can tap into the following effective tools:

Lost and Found at the Medi/Spa

I was visiting my parents and someone who does car detailing came knocking on the door asking me if I was interested in getting my car detailed. I thought, "Yes, I need it done," so I agreed to his price and a few hours later my car looked brand new again. He did a great job! I was so happy! A few months passed and I was teaching a seminar. I always have attendees in my car, so I thought it would be great to detail my car again. I looked everywhere for his card but could not find it. That led me to think about why he did not bother to contact me again. So, what does this story have to do with reactivating lost medi/spa clients? Everything!

Many times we think that clients do not come back because they did not like us. But that is not usually true! You see, we all have very busy lives. We run here and there. We attend this and that, and unless we are reminded of things, you know the saying, "Out of sight, out of mind."

Your clients may not be coming back because you probably did not contact them or reach out to invite them back. Here are a couple of strategies you can implement to help you find your lost clients and increase your revenue.

There is a term in business called "attrition." Attrition refers to the percentage of clients you lose or those who become inactive.

Normally, medi/spa leaders write off missing clients as lost clients or don't even track their attrition rate. But you shouldn't. Those clients are not lost, they're inactive! It's up to you to reactivate them and get them to re-visit your medi/spa on a regular basis.

As a medi/spa entrepreneur, this is an important task to focus on. It's a fact: it costs more time and money to generate a new client than to bring back an old one. Statistics show that over 55% of inactive clients become active again if they are contacted again! 55%! That's five or more out of every 10 lost clients who would come back to your medi/spa if you just reach out to them.

Strategy to turn inactive clients from lost to found:

1. Personalized email
2. Send them a newsletter
3. A direct mail campaign
4. An invitation to an event
5. A de-stress recipe card
6. "A Gift for You!" campaign
7. Enter to win
8. Invite them to a "Let's Reconnect" event

Why Medi/Spa Memberships and Loyalty Programs?

Membership and loyalty programs have been in existence for years in companies such as Sam's, Costco, AAA, churches, country clubs, and airlines. They have utilized them over and over very successfully.

Now, even the medi/spa industry is on the band wagon! In 2009, Massage Envy opened their first location offering massage memberships, and they now have over 1,000 locations. It proves that the U.S. population loves to belong to clubs and be members of an organization. Now there are several other brands launching similar membership programs. I often get asked, "How can I compete with those types of businesses?"

You can compete with chains by creating unique membership and loyalty programs. There are many benefits to offering membership and loyalty programs. First, let's identify the difference between the two.

A membership program is where a person agrees to pay the medi/spa a certain amount per month to receive a treatment. The monthly fee is being charged automatically. A loyalty program is where you give your clients rewards for doing business with you over and over. Ideally, you should have both. The membership ensures a steady cash flow and the loyalty program ensures retention.

To help you, here are eight essential steps to launch a unique membership program.

1) **Design Your Program:** Decide on the type of membership program you want to offer. Don't get stuck on massage only.

Remember, you want to be unique. You can offer a de-stress program with massages and other medi/spa treatments, an acne program either for adults or teens, a wellness and nutrition program, or an anti-aging program. Be creative!

2) **The Right Price:** Don't worry about being the least expensive. Focus on the type of experience you offer and introduce added value benefits. You won't win if you compete on price alone.

3) **Membership Management System:** Having a membership management software system is a must. Don't attempt to launch a program without it. This will assist you with member usage tracking, retention, attrition, and overall success.

4) **Monthly Payment:** Automated payment processing capabilities are also a very important management step. Be aware of failed payments. Have a collection process in place to avoid member late payment or delinquency.

5) **Membership Guidelines:** Have FAQs (Frequently Asked Questions) and answers to all the "what if" questions such as accruals, cancellations, multiple use, payments, etc.

6) **Marketing and Launching your Membership:** Create all your marketing materials, posters, flyers, membership cards, website updates, agreements, brochures, etc. in advance!

7) **Team Training:** Selling the membership program requires a team effort. Make sure you train your team and set performance expectations and rewards to ensure your success.

8) **Track Member Usage:** To ensure a long lifetime value,

make sure you track usage. You don't want members to miss their usage. If they do, the likelihood of canceling is greater. You want them to get into the habit of using their membership on a regular basis. It's wise to have automated reminder messages to keep members engaged.

Loyalty Program

The best loyalty programs are simple and easy to understand. The airline model where clients earn a point for every mile traveled is an excellent practice. You can do the same and offer one point for every dollar your guest spends. The more they spend, the more points they accumulate.

To redeem points earned, you can create a brochure with items they can purchase with their points. For example, you can have branded items such as spa robes, neck wraps, water bottles, wellness books, and other fun things that are rare and can't be found in stores.

If you are not offering a membership and/or loyalty program, I encourage you to do both. Tap into this great revenue stream to increase your retention and profits!

Dori Recommends....

To help you with your business you can tap into the following effective tools:

10 Steps to Creating Your Membership USB

Two Strategies to Ignite Your Business!

Boost your revenue by implementing the following:

1. Drive Men to the medi/spa by tapping into your current female database.

Did you know that June is Men's Health Month? You can launch a Men's Health Campaign and boost your male traffic. Take advantage of this opportunity and start planning now.

The women to men ratio of medi/spa goers is 80% women to 20% men. You can tap into your female database and launch an entire campaign to market to the men in their lives. Your campaign will include an event to introduce them to your medi/spa and all the benefits they will gain from your products and treatments.

During the event, you can have a speaker talking about how men can be healthier, how to look younger, or how to de-stress; whatever topics you would like to focus on. This will bring forth the importance of visiting the medi/spa and the role your business can play in helping men obtain or maintain a healthier lifestyle and look their very best.

If you have the Secrets to Successful Event Planning USB (at: https://www.insparationmanagement.com/shop/cd-ten-steps-to-developing-launching-spa-memberships/ you will need to listen to it and implement the step by step strategy on how to host a very successful event. You can make thousands of dollars in just three hours. If you don't have the USB, get it now!

Create a program for men and turn them into regular medi/spa goers! This will boost your revenue exponentially this summer and beyond!

2. Create a New Summer Program – Take a Medi/Spacation Instead of a Vacation

Some people can't take vacations. So why not show them how they can take a Medi/Spacation?

Develop a summer program to include a few trips to the spa with a specific Medi/Spacation menu from which they can choose. For example, they can visit your spa every two weeks during the summer and receive any treatments from your Medi/Spacation menu.

They can commit to a two or three-month Medi/Spacation program and you can charge them a flat monthly fee. You may want to even consider having two or three different price points: low, medium, and high to fit everyone's budget.

This will encourage your client base to visit more frequently and take advantage of this specially priced program offered only in the summer.

Economical Self-Marketing Strategy

Often, I see medi/spas place "your next appointment" on the back of the business card. This is ok for in-medi/spa use to help your client remember their next appointment but do the following to self-market and generate new clients.

Print new business cards and place a promotion on the back and your information on the front. Keep them with you at all times. Any time you are around people, introduce yourself and pass out the card. Always promote yourself! If you don't do it, who will?

On the back of the card, you can print:

A Gift For You...
A Complimentary Eye Treatment
With Your First Facial

Here is a script sample. Let's assume you are at the bank, a social event, or buying something from the mall. Pull out your card and say something like this:

"I noticed how hard you are working. My name is _____ and I am a professional therapist working at _____ medi/spa. Here is my card and on the back is a gift for you to come and see me. Let me take care of you. We have a beautiful medi/spa for you to relax and recharge in. I look forward to seeing you! Make sure to ask for me when you make your appointment."

Choose whatever you would like to offer as a gift. We recommend you do a card for each department.

For example, the massage department can have:

A Gift For You...
A Body Scrub
With Your First Massage

The hair department can have:

A Gift For You...
A Complimentary Hair Conditioning Treatment
With Your First Hair Cut

This is the most economical method to self-market. Teach the entire team how to do this and watch your business grow!

Driving More Male Clientele to Your Medi/Spa

For many years, the ratio of women to men visiting medi/spas was at 80 to 20. According to a recent report (by ISPA) men represent 39% of medi/spa visitors.

It seems that men are spending money on products beyond the traditional shaving accessories and deodorants. They are now buying skin care, hair care, and bath products. They want products that are specifically targeted for them rather than using their significant other's shower gels and body lotions.

If that's the case, why are more men not visiting medi/spas? They are not visiting medi/spas because medi/spa leaders are marketing to men the same way they are marketing to women, and we know how well that's working! If you want to attract more men to your medi/spa, you need to change your marketing strategies, your positioning, and your offer.

When marketing to men, keep in mind that, to men, looking good is looking strong, confident, authoritative, and adventurous. Men tend to decide quicker than women exactly what it is they want. Men are not browsers. The male motto for shopping is, "Get what I want and move on." Men shop for what they need *now*. Men like simple and to the point; just tell them what problem this treatment will solve and what the results are and they will buy.

Here are six new marketing strategies you can implement to help you drive more men to your medi/spa and expand your market share and your revenue:

1. Medi/Spa Menu

Problem: Most medi/spa menus focus on female treatment. You may find one treatment, maybe two, for men. The menu content, feel, and image are catering to women. This immediately reduces the likelihood of a man coming to you. You are not speaking to them. That's why we have both Vogue magazine and GQ. They each target a different market.

Solution: Create a man-specific treatment menu. Use colors, copy, and style that is appealing to men. It can be a small trifold and may include treatments similar to those on the women's menu, but they must be described differently. Descriptions must target the male population and speak to them, directly addressing their problems and offering solutions. Name your treatments in ways to attract their attention. Don't just say male manicure. Try something like "Hand Detailing." Instead of saying "Facial for Men" try "Executive Facial," etc. Copy is key when creating a menu for men.

2. Website

Problem: Most medi/spa websites feature mainly women in their images and with their treatment descriptions. Many are still talking about pampering... this type of website drives men away rather than capturing their attention.

Solution: Create a men-only area on your website so they can go and discover all the treatments available for men. Make sure your home page is neutral and features both men and women.

3. On Hold Message

Problem: Most on hold messages don't advertise that the XYZ medi/spa is the ideal place for both men and women to relax, de-stress, and rejuvenate. This is a missed opportunity.

Solution: Create a new on hold message making it clear that you are a "unisex medi/spa" that provides treatments and programs for both men and women.

4. Medi/Spa Positioning

Problem: Men have different needs than women. Currently, most medi/spas cater to women.

Solution: In order to tap into the male market, medi/spas need to have a clear understanding of what men's needs are. Create a survey or focus group to clearly understand what your male target market needs. This will help you reposition your offering and your medi/spa to attract the male market and increase revenue.

5. Advertising

Problem: Email campaigns, newsletters, ads, and other promotional materials are, again, normally geared toward women.

Solution: Create marketing materials that target both men and women.

6. Medi/Spa Ambiance

Problem: Medi/Spa colors, reading material in the relaxation lounge, décor, guest attire, etc., normally have a feminine feel.

Solution: I am not saying redecorate your medi/spa, but maybe you can create a special area where men will feel more comfortable.

Here are some additional strategies you may want to consider helping you attract more men to your medi/spa:

a. Consider designating certain hours during the week to take only male clients to satisfy the men who don't necessarily care to see women while at the medi/spa.
b. Create a male-only membership program.
c. Offer an image consultation and style consultation.
d. Keep the menu simple. Focus on problems and solutions, and the benefits of the treatments.
e. Ask your female clients to refer one man each. Provide them with the men's menu to pass on with a complimentary consultation.
f. Recommend products, educate them on how to use them, and share expected results.
g. Men have different interests than women. Make sure your therapist can carry on a conversation about male topics such as sports, cars, business, etc.
h. Go where the metrosexual males are. Defined as affluent, urban males who pay more attention to appearance and grooming than was once considered masculine, they have made grooming regimens more familiar to men. Go to where they are. Visit country clubs and fitness centers to invite them to visit your medi/spa and receive a complimentary consultation.

Now is the time to reposition your medi/spa and earn your part of the male market share.

Dori Recommends....

To help you with your business you can tap into the following effective tools:

Menu Development Dos & Don'ts

Rejuvenate Your Business

In the medi/spa industry, we are always talking about rejuvenating our clients. Rarely do I hear conversations about rejuvenating our businesses. This thought came to me as I attended one of our clients' grand openings last week. It was a great event! The mayor showed up for the ribbon cutting ceremony. They had a lot of TV and radio media; about 250 people attended. Needless to say, a lot of buzz and excitement was generated. Since the event, their phones have not stopped ringing! I keep checking in with them and they are still reserving appointments like mad. Why am I telling you this? Because hosting events is one of my favorite things to do to generate new business. So why not rejuvenate your business and host a grand re-opening event?

Here are some economical steps to rejuvenate your business:

1. Paint
You can enhance your medi/spa's appearance for the price of one facial. $100 worth of paint will give your medi/spa a fresh and renewed look. Even if you don't paint the entire place, painting a few accents on walls will change the entire look and feel of the medi/spa.

2. New bed covers and scarves
I received many e-mails asking me where I bought the bed scarf in the picture I used in one of my blogs; many of you loved it! This is a table runner. You can find them anywhere

for about $18/$25. Talk about a fresh look! All you need is a cover and a nice scarf and you've just rejuvenated your treatment rooms, and you did it for about $30 each!

3. Merchandising

Your medi/spa boutique can look so much better with some props mixed in with your products. Stop lining up products one next to another; give your shelves some personality. You can buy props at Home Goods, Pier One, etc. Watch for sales and buy them when they are reduced. Your medi/spa boutique should entice guests to look around and spend money.

4. Menu options

Add a new treatment to your menu; fill a void you may not be fulfilling now. This will give you something to talk about to the media during your grand re-opening. You don't have to reprint your menu; give the new treatment or program its own positioning. This will save a lot of money unless it is time to reprint new menus anyway.

5. Team image

Upgrade your team's image with a uniformed look. Again, it does not have to be expensive. It can even be a nice t-shirt with your logo on it with new name tags, and your entire team will have a new image.

Once your business rejuvenation is complete, plan your grand re-opening event. Enjoy the buzz! Your event will generate all kinds of new opportunities and get your phone ringing off the hook!

We offer a coaching program called "CoachMe." It's held once every month. It's a group coaching call where we discuss different topics to help medi/spa professionals with their businesses. Last week, I had one of our clients as a special guest on the call, Natalie Spencer from the Renaissance European Day Spa. I met Natalie almost three years ago and we have been working together ever since. Our firm helped them plan their grand re-opening where they generated $180K in fitness and spa sales in six hours. They had just remodeled their facility. Their event is still generating revenue! You can do this, too. Get motivated and rejuvenate your business now!

Dori Recommends….

To help you with your business you can tap into the following effective tools:

CoachMe Series   **Visit
CoachMeOnDemand.com**

Focusing on the Three RRRs

Entrepreneurs are always looking for ways to increase revenue and enhance performance. How about you? Are you looking for ways to boost your business this year? You can by focusing on the three RRR's. What are the three RRR's?

a. Referrals
b. Retention
c. Reactivation

We can spend all day talking about the three RRR's, but let me give you few strategies that you can apply immediately that will positively impact your business.

1. Referrals: I don't know if you are a business owner, solo-preneur, or a doctor reading this, but no matter what your position is you need to focus on generating referrals. Did you know you could double your business if every one of your clients simply referred one person? Need I say more about how important focusing on referral is? Go ahead, launch a referral campaign and gain new clients.

I was getting my coffee the other day and there was a long line, so I started talking to the person behind me and it turned out that she was a hairstylist and worked in a medi/spa. So I asked how it was going and she started whining about how slow it was. Behind us, two more ladies joined the conversation. Instead of whining all they had to say was, "We are doing great and we stay very busy... here is my card if you or someone else you know is looking for a hairstylist. I have a couple of openings in my schedule and would love to help!"

That's self-promotion and referring people to your business. So please don't tell people you are slow or whine. That's not good for you or the industry. Focus on the positive! There are many people that could use your services and your products, so focus on asking for referrals and watch your capacity grow.

2. Retention: When I ask medi/spa leaders what their medi/spa retention rate is, many guestimate at the answer or don't know at all. How about you? Do you know your retention rate? I hope so... Retention is a direct reflection to the type of experience you deliver. If you deliver a great experience, people will come back. If you deliver an indifferent experience, they won't come back. It's that simple. How good is your experience?

I was a secret shopper last week and I had a one-handed massage. Have you had one of those? It's terrible... Will I go back to that medi/spa? NO. Assess your experience and track your retention rate. Gather a focus group, survey your clients, put in place effective guest feedback forms, and look closely at your retention rate.

3. Reactivation: Have you reached out to bring guests back that you have not seen in a while? You need to launch a reactivation campaign. Dig deep and gather a list of all the people who have not visited your medi/spa in a while and invite them back. Or reach out and find out why they haven't been back, or host a reunion event. There are so many things you can do to bring defectors back. Hold a team meeting and brainstorm with them to create your reactivation campaign. This will benefit everyone one on the team and help increase your revenue.

Talk about the three RRR's with your team and focus on them to make this year your best year yet.

Dori Recommends….

To help you with your business you can tap into the following effective tools:

Recipes For Success Series

First Impressions – How Good is Yours?

To me, first impressions are everything!

Recently I visited a local medi/spa and the first thing that I saw upon entering was the medi/spa receptionist. Let me say that this was no ordinary medi/spa receptionist; this young lady was definitely someone I will never forget. Not only was her hair an unnatural pinkish red color (you know what I'm talking about), but even more stunning was the bright pink lip-shaped tattoos scattering her décolleté and neck region. To make things even more interesting, she looked extremely unapproachable, never bothered to make eye contact with me or to greet me. Needless to say my visit was brief; after looking over the product shelves, I grabbed the service menu and left. Was this the upscale medi/spa that they solicited themselves as? I don't think so! The popular warning of, "You never get a second chance to make a good first impression," really does stand true.

It got me thinking that no matter how much we might think that we are non-judgmental, every one of us is guilty of making snap judgments about people and places we visit. It's estimated that it only takes three seconds for us to make an initial judgment about somebody we meet for the very first time. What impression are people forming about your place of business?

When clients walk through the door and are greeted by the receptionist or they call your medi/spa and the receptionist answers the telephone, they are immediately forming an opinion about your products, services, and your overall facility. Your receptionists must represent your medi/spa through their appearance, behavior, attitude, business manners, and communication skills. No matter how busy the reception area is, the entire medi/spa counts on its receptionists to always project a professional image and make a great first and lasting impression.

Do your medi/spa receptionists reflect a professional image for your medi/spa? Remember, the reception area is a major profit center. Is this person helping to increase your revenue or are they potentially hurting your bottom line? As a medi/spa owner or manager, you must continually evaluate your front-line team. Below are eight key performance objectives that a manager or owner should measure and expect from their receptionists.

1. Portray a professional medi/spa image: uniform or professional attire
2. Above average communication skills and word selection
3. Positive non-verbal communication skills: body language and eye contact
4. Effective listening skills
5. Problem-solving ability and guest satisfaction
6. Telephone mastery
7. Exceptional product and service knowledge
8. Organizational skills including work space

You *cannot* afford a bad first impression. Create a good first impression and your clientele numbers will flourish and so will your overall revenue. Give a bad first impression and you will continue to fight an uphill battle. Take a moment and assess your first impression and improve upon it.

Seven Steps to Transform Your Medi/Spa Makeup Business

Many medi/spas offer makeup, but in most cases, it's stuck in a corner as if it were an afterthought. No major focus is usually applied to ensure the success of this department. Often, I wonder why medi/spas even offer makeup if it's just going to sit there collecting dust. It's time for change! Here are seven easy steps to turn your makeup studio into a mega revenue source!

1. Proper Positioning
Makeup can generate a large sum of income when it's positioned properly. Your makeup studio should be located in a well-lit area with a makeup mirror and a proper makeup chair. It should be clean, attractive, organized, and inviting for your clients to experience.

2. Develop a Makeup Menu
This is a BIG missed opportunity. Normally, consumers just see one phrase or paragraph within the menu about makeup. Instead, you should provide them with a rack card or a separate insert describing all of your makeup offerings, enticing them to purchase repeatedly.

Here is a sample of what your makeup menu should include:

Teen Lessons
A large segment of your clientele is women in their 40s or 50s who have teenage girls in need of your help. Launch a campaign to all the moms so you can help their daughters learn to properly apply makeup and teach them which makeup to purchase. You can even turn it into a mother/daughter lesson!

Special Occasion Application

We all have special occasions to attend such as birthdays, anniversaries, parties, and events where we want to make a great impression. Unfortunately, most of your clients probably are not aware that you offer special occasion services; therefore, both you and your clients are missing out on great opportunities.

Wedding Makeup

This is a very big business to tap into. You have the bride and the entire wedding party to help. You can offer pre-wedding programs for the bride and her bridal party. You can even do a program for the bachelorette party! If you have a salon, you can also do their hair. Offer complete wedding programs. Again, if your menu does not list or describe wedding programs, you are missing out on this HUGE business opportunity.

Expert Makeover & Seasonal Refresher

We all could use a makeover! Offer a seasonal refresher to help your clients stay looking their best through seasonal changes. They should experience a seasonal refresher at least once a quarter.

After Treatment Mini Application

No woman wants to leave the medi/spa without makeup after a facial. By offering a mini application, it will set you apart from the competition and provide the opportunity to sell your makeup!

Makeup Products

And, of course, you need to tell your clients about your makeup products and why they are so great!

Create your menu. Have a hard copy and post it on your website. See your makeup sales grow!

3. Marketing Your Makeup

Any business requires marketing to succeed, and makeup is no exception. Here are some marketing essentials for you to implement.

Plan a makeup event at least once a quarter. Launch makeup promotions, offer a gift with a purchase, feature added value. Create a Discovery Makeup Station so your clients can sample your makeup. Department stores sell billions of dollars annually because they allow women to test products; you must do the same. Get the rest of the team to cross-market to help build your makeup clientele. You can also tap into upgrade opportunities such as lashes, facials, and injectables. Don't forget about all the tools your clients will need: brushes, sponges, cleansers, eye makeup remover, and so on.

4. Team Makeup Training

Training the team is essential to your success. There are several schools that can help train your team to improve their makeup skills and learn about the latest colors and trends. It is worth the investment if you are serious about your makeup business.

5. Business Tools to Sell Products

One of the strategies I teach clients is how to use a "Guest Discovery Form" to learn about the clients' needs. It helps achieve the look or the results your clients are looking for. It should be utilized by makeup artists to discuss your clients' needs and serve as a communication tool leading to recommendations.

The other essential tool is a face chart to be utilized as a closing tool. You can show the client all the colors and products you just used on them or the colors you are recommending. It helps close the sale by having them see all the products and the price total so they commit to the new look.

6. Selling Your Makeup Products

To maximize your makeup business, establish targets and goals. Take the time to calculate the number of clients who visit your facility on a daily, weekly, and monthly basis. Set targets for how much revenue you want to average per guest. Additionally, launch performance-based compensation to motivate your team.

7. Measuring Results

Don't forget to measure performance. Keep coaching the team until they reach the level of performance you are striving for!

Makeup can truly be a great revenue source for your business, but you need to give it the attention it deserves. I encourage you to implement these seven steps and watch your makeup business soar!

The Menu Makeover

Innovation and creativity are essential to maintaining your competitive edge, ensuring growth, and increasing client retention. Medi/Spa suppliers are constantly striving to discover new ingredients, manufacturing processes, equipment, and product ideas to help consumers look and feel their very best. As a medi/spa leader, it is your responsibility to stay abreast of all the new and exciting treatments that are introduced by suppliers and to select the right offerings for your clients. Frequently I am asked, "How often should I change my menu?" Ideally you should revise and assess your menu once per year.

Discover:
- What treatments are selling and which ones are not
- The needs of your target market by conducting surveys
- The most and least popular price points
- The most popular treatment duration
- The most popular retail products

Once you've done your assessment, you will be able to make a wise decision to modify your menu.

Here are some of the most popular trends to keep in mind when renewing your menu.

For Face
(Esthetic Oncology)
This medi/spa offering is gaining popularity. Estheticians can get certified and learn how to perform facials on cancer

patients. Offering this type of treatment will set you apart from other medi/spas, compassionately addressing the needs of people who truly require specialized help.

For Body

Slimming body treatments are ideal for any medi/spa menu. Whether you use equipment or simply a body wrap, you will fulfill the needs of many consumers who are seeking to lose few inches here and there and want to slim down. Offering slimming body treatments will fulfill the needs of a large target market, helping position you as a results-driven medi/spa.

For Hair

We always hear about anti-aging treatments for face and body, but not very often do we hear about it for hair. Offer an anti-aging hair treatment and increase your revenue per guest. Everyone's hair goes through changes. Addressing those changes will generate more revenue while increasing guest satisfaction.

For Medi-Spa

(Wellness Programs)

Weight management is one of the biggest problems facing our nation. If you operate a medi-spa, go beyond offering just Botox, fillers, laser hair removal, etc. Include an effective weight management program with healthy living coaching and provide this much-needed program in your community.

For Nails, Hands, *and* Feet

Like hair, we rarely offer an upgrade opportunity for anti-aging hand treatments. This can easily be recommended to almost every person who is receiving a mani or pedi treatment. Use any anti-aging brush-on mask from your facial line and offer it as an upgrade or as a regular anti-aging manicure treatment.

For Wellness

Consider including energy healing. Energy healing comes in many forms. You can offer Reiki, Shiatsu, acupuncture, reflexology, and sound therapy. When these modalities are paired with massage, energy healing can facilitate a deeper sense of relaxation and well-being.

Retail

If you want to increase your retail sales, consider creating a beauty or skin care bar. Give your clients the opportunity to try and sample *your* products. Department stores have been doing this for years and are very successful at it. Yet in the medi/spa business, we keep everything locked up or put away. If you want to sell more products, you've got to make them accessible to your clients.

Medi/Spa Gifts

Everyone sells gift cards but rarely do I see retail products as part of the offering. We have implemented this strategy with many clients and the results are amazing! Create gift card packages including treatments *and* products to increase your sales exponentially.

Memberships

Offering a membership program at your medi/spa is a great way to increase retention and produce a guaranteed monthly income. People love to belong. Look at the fitness industry: they don't have a la carte visits, you have to join. Why not do the same! It takes a little planning, the right pricing, software to manage your membership program, and a good team to sell it. Memberships will maximize your revenue and increase your retention. Best of all, your clients will gain the results they are seeking!

Loyalty

Loyalty programs are great! Again, look at the airline industry: they have been doing loyalty programs for years. I have the pleasure of speaking at many tradeshows and when I ask the question, "Who has a loyalty program?" very few hands go up. Why? It's not rocket science. Implementing a loyalty program will increase your retention and reward your clients for being true to you and your brand!

To complete the menu makeover process, do a survey or conduct a focus group meeting to learn more about your target market's needs. Then create a menu that ideally addresses those needs. It's a win-win for everyone!

How Effective is your Medi/Spa Menu?

What is the difference between a menu and a pamphlet? Which one will help you sell your services more?

A *menu* is a multi-page booklet offering your guests treatment descriptions, information about the medi/spa, and what their experience will be like when they arrive. A good menu excites and compels the guest to reserve a package or a treatment.

A *pamphlet (or price list)* simply states the names of the treatments and their prices.

Many studies have been conducted to research why people buy. The results indicate that people buy because the products or services:

1. will **solve** a problem or concern
2. provide a **benefit**
3. are recommended by someone they **like** and **trust**
4. have **value** to them
5. produce the **results** they want and deliver what has been promised

Menu mistakes to be replaced with strategies to *sell* your services:

1. Our: I find the word "our" in many menus. It's not about you and your medi/spa. It's all about the guest! The verbiage should focus on them. Go through your menu and website and count how many times you have used the word "our." Replace them with "your" or rephrase the sentence so that the focus will be on the guest and their experience.

2. First Page: So many times, I see the medi/spa's policy on the inside first page of the menu. BIG mistake! The first page should have your welcome message and a short paragraph about the medi/spa's story. The "how to guidelines" page should be the *very last page* within the menu. Also, try replacing the overused and unfriendly "cancellation policy" with "Rescheduling your Experience." Who wants to hear about your policies when they are thinking about a medi/spa experience?

3. Small Font: Your clientele needs to be able to read the menu. Remember, baby boomers! Choose a font that's easy to read and avoid the cute or artsy ones.

4. Images: Remember, we're selling emotional connections. Be sure to include pictures in your menu with people in them.

5. Pricing: The price list should be a card insert. This way if you change your prices, you won't have to replace the entire menu.

6. Too Many Treatment Options: Keeping your menu simple is a key factor to selling your services. When you overload guests with too many options, they will not take action.

7. Book Your Service: I see this phrase too often. Consider replacing it with "reserve your medi/spa experience."

8. Measuring the Menu's Performance: Run the following reports to discover how effective your treatment selections are and make adjustments accordingly.
- Best sellers
- Least demanding
- Most popular price point

- Least popular price point
- Packages vs. a la carte

9. Changing and Updating Your Menu: Your menu needs to change at least once per year, especially in today's economy. If you are still talking about pampering, you are killing your business. Shift your menu wording to include the latest buzz words:
- de-stress
- balance
- health
- wellness programs

10. Focus Group: When you are thinking about making menu changes, ask a group of your loyal clientele who represent the majority of your market to participate as a focus group. Share with them what you are planning to change and have them experience the treatments or try the products you're considering. Afterwards, discuss price point and collect their feedback. Review your information and make your decisions.

Summary: How to Structure a Menu that SELLS

Page:
1. *Welcome* – your medi/spa story
2. *Customized Programs* – signature treatments
3. *Anti-Aging*
4. *Facial Options*
5. *Massage Therapy*
6. *Body Treatment Contour*
7. Boutique
8. How-to guidelines

Remember: Your menu tells clients who you are! Investing in your menu is well worth the time and money.

Six Steps to a Profitable Acne Program

Acne is one of the biggest missed opportunities within the medi/spa industry. This potentially huge revenue stream is rarely explored within medi/spas. Currently on most medi/spa menus, you will find a deep cleansing facial or a teen facial, an acne treatment, etc. These are typically positioned as one a la carte treatment. The problem is that acne cannot be solved with one treatment. To clear acne, the person must participate in an acne program or membership lasting many months to gain and maintain the results they are looking for. Here you will learn six steps to develop, position, and market your acne program to increase guest satisfaction and generate more revenue.

1. Identify Your Acne Program Target Market
The largest segment of the medi/spa industry's clientele is women in the age group of 40 to 60. Most of them have teenagers. This is one of the biggest missed target markets. The parents, who are your clients, already like you and trust you. They have children with skin problems that you can help. Identify those clients with teenage children by doing a "Getting To Know You survey." This will provide a targeted list to market your teen acne program.

2. Develop Your Acne Program
Identify which equipment, result-driven products, and frequency they will need to participate in to develop your acne program. The clients InSPAration Management has helped implement acne programs that work best is when the teen visits the medi/spa twice per month. In addition to the medi/spa visit, they will need to adhere to a home care regimen that should be part of your program. Keep in mind that this is *not* a turn down the lights type of experience. It's

a clinical and results-driven program. The price for the program needs to be reasonable for a parent to want to invest in a monthly program for their child. Depending on your area, you can charge anywhere from $99 to $149 per month. This amount is automatically charged on a monthly basis to a credit card.

3. Create Your Marketing Material
Now that you have developed your program, you will need to create your marketing material. It takes preparation to properly launch a new treatment and/or products. You will need a flyer, email blast, posters, buttons, website update, social media site postings, etc. Come up with a name for the program and an entire marketing strategy to grab your consumer's attention. Entice them to learn more and sign up for your acne program.

4. Team Training for Technical and Sales
The success of your acne program lies in the hands of your team. They will have to be very skilled in performing acne treatments and must be able to promote it. Have them wear buttons with a statement saying, "Want Clear Skin? Ask Us How!" This will open the conversation, allow the team to discuss the program, and sign the client up. You may want to offer a team bonus for programs sold.

5. Launch Your Acne Program
Once you have all of your marketing material, treatment protocols, products, and your system set up, you are ready to launch. You can begin promoting through your marketing mix and also by hosting an event to introduce your acne program. Your event should be fun and educational. The theme can be, "Bring Your Teen and Their Friends to Discover How to Have Blemish-Free Skin." This event is a great opportunity to explain the program and get people registered.

6. Measure Results and Refine Your Plan

Measuring results will ensure program success. It is wise to document progress and obtain testimonials from the results you were able to achieve. You will be able to use testimonials to help promote the program continually. The other important fact to measure is your member count. How many people do you want in your program? 50, 100, or more? Set a target for the number of members you would like to reach. Make sure that you are doing all the marketing needed to help reach your goal.

If you are looking for ways to boost your income, implementing an acne program or other programs will increase retention, satisfaction, and revenue! You can be like Beth Pestotnik, CEO of Skin Essentials in CO. She launched her acne program six months ago and now has over 100 members paying $95 per month. That's over $9,000 of guaranteed income per month!

I encourage you to remove the a la carte mentality, focus on programs, and have your best year ever!

Five Steps to Generating Revenue Through Guest Consultation

The guest is the most important individual to the success of any medi/spa business. How we take care of guests while they are in the medi/spa makes the difference between whether they come back or disappear forever.

When I ask medi/spa professionals why they chose a career in the medi/spa industry, the most popular answer I hear is, "To help people!" Yet when a new guest visits a medi/spa, they normally are asked to select a treatment from the menu and then simply receive that treatment without any discussion about it. Sometimes I intentionally select the wrong treatment from the menu to see if the therapist will recommend something else more ideally suited for me. Rarely do I hear a recommendation.

Why? Because in most cases, medi/spa professionals don't take the time to conduct a proper guest consultation. To me, the guest consultation is the most important step of the entire experience. The guest consultation ensures that medi/spa professionals are going to provide the guest with exactly what they need, address their challenges, and deliver the results they are looking for. Without a consultation, we are disappointing guests and hurting our retention rate.

If you want to increase your guest satisfaction, retention rate, and your income, we suggest you keep reading and implement the following five steps to generating revenue through guest consultation.

1. **Schedule Time to Conduct a Detailed Consultation**

   When you have a new client, you should always schedule a consultation first in order to learn and discover their concerns and needs. It's wise to have the receptionist reserve time for a treatment and a consultation. Have the therapist decide which treatment is ideal for the guest once a consultation is performed. To do this, your receptionist must be trained how to present the consultation appointment and make the reservation for it.

2. **Identify Guest Concerns**

   To identify the guest's concerns, you can use analysis equipment for face, body, and hair depending on the type of treatments you offer. We found that when people see their skin care concerns with their own eyes, they are more motivated to take action on your recommendations. You can also use consultation forms; just make sure the form includes problems that guests could be experiencing with their face, body, nails, etc. The guest will mark the concerns they have and that will provide you the opportunity to make the appropriate recommendations. You should focus on solving their problems via your menu.

3. **Develop a Customized Treatment Program**

   To address people's concerns and gain results, it normally requires multiple treatments. As a medi/spa professional, you should recommend a series of treatments, not just one.

One treatment is not going to produce the results your guests are looking for.

4. **Recommend a Home Care Program**

At the end of the first treatment, take the time to help your guests by recommending a home care regimen. Home care is an important part of gaining results. Don't cheat your guests out of your professional advice or rob your family from the additional income you could be generating from home care products.

5. **Measure Results**

Since the goal is to recommend a series of treatments with your consultation, it's important to measure results and gain a testimonial from happy clients. You can take before and after pictures or document conditions and measure improvements. Whichever method you choose, make sure you gain a raving fan to help build your business.

Conducting a guest consultation is truly the most important function of your medi/spa. It is the foundation of the entire experience. Don't dismiss it, embrace it! Implementing the guest consultation process with every new client will help you increase client satisfaction and your income!

Dori Recommends….

To help you with your business you can tap into the following effective tools:

Success with Guest Consultation Manual and Audio

Four Easy Steps to Evaluating Your Guests' Medi/Spa Experience

Did you know…

- For one unsatisfied guest who complains, 26 other unhappy guests say nothing and 24 won't come back.
- The average guest who experiences a problem with your business will tell 9 to 10 people about it.
- When complaints are addressed quickly, 70% to 95% will do business with the company again. (*Source: the Dept. of Commerce*)

Your retention rate is a direct reflection of the quality of the experience you are delivering. Have you calculated your medi/spa's retention rate lately? How high is it?

Several InSPAration Management clients are asking, "How do we create a guest feedback form?" Keep reading and you will discover four steps to measure your medi/spa's guest experience. Capture your guests' feedback in order to improve your guest experience and retention rate!

Step 1: Create your Guest Feedback Form

I experienced:
      Facial
      Massage
      Body treatments
      Injectables
      Other _____

Reservation Rating

1. Reserving my medi/spa experience with the medi/spa concierge was hassle free, informative, and conducted efficiently and professionally.

Disagree   Somewhat Agree   Agree   Strongly agree

Support Team
2. The medi/spa's support team was professional, courteous, and attended to all my needs.
Disagree   Somewhat Agree   Agree   Strongly agree

Medi/Spa Therapists
3. My therapist was highly skilled and my treatments were performed with attention to detail, exceeding my expectations.
Disagree   Somewhat Agree   Agree   Strongly agree

The Medi/Spa
4. The medi/spa ambiance, decor, music, and cleanliness made the spa a warm, soothing, and inviting place to be.
Disagree   Somewhat Agree   Agree   Strongly agree

Medi/Spa Products
5. The medi/spa products and treatments were of high quality. I loved the feelings, sensations, and the results.
Disagree   Somewhat Agree   Agree   Strongly agree

Overall Medi/Spa Experience
6. My overall medi/spa experience exceeded my expectations.
Disagree   Somewhat Agree   Agree   Strongly agree

Referral
7. I would refer the medi/spa to my family and friends.
Yes   No

8. What can we do to enhance the medi/spa experience further?

Step 2: Form Placement and Type
A. On your website
B. In print at the front desk
C. Email format

Step 3: Special offers
At check out, you can offer your guests the following:
1. Complete the form and receive a complimentary enhancement treatment when reserving now.
2. Complete the form and enter to win a complimentary massage.

Step 4: What to Do with the Information
Use the results to make necessary adjustments. Set up training and coaching sessions to correct certain medi/spa conditions and team behaviors. Remember, you can't fix what you don't measure.

Dori Recommends....

Invite InSPAration Management to conduct a secret shopping assessment in your medi/spa and receive recommendations to improve your guest experience.

Weaving Wellness into Your Medi/Spa Menu

Are you looking to expand your menu offering and venture into wellness? As the medi/spa industry evolves, more and more medi/spas are making the shift into wellness and are expanding their revenue streams. There are many wellness program options you can consider. Here are a few:

- Nutrition or Weight Management
- Stress Management
- Chinese Medicine
- Life Coaching & Mapping
- Integrative Medicine

To properly create and launch a wellness program, it takes time and effort. The following six steps will help you navigate through the process:

1. Survey Your Target Market and Your Database
2. Plan and Develop the Program
3. Create Marketing Material to Launch
4. Manage the Program
5. Measure Results
6. Team Contribution

1. **Survey Your Target Market and Your Database**
   This is an essential step to determine the type of wellness program your clients or target market are interested in. Do a survey and ask key questions to help discover their wellness needs. The questions must be decisive so you can gain important data. Another option is to gather a focus group of loyal clients. Inform them of the type of program you are considering and at what price point to see if they agree to

your offering. Surveying prior to developing your wellness program will save considerable time and money. Don't skip this very important step!

2. **Plan and Develop the Program**

   Now that you know the type of program you want to offer, it's time to begin planning. You need to map out the who, what, where, when, and why of the project. This is a time consuming but necessary process to ensure a great program that produces positive results. Remember, you don't have to do everything yourself. When you map out the project, assign different tasks to different people on your team to help expedite the process.

   Another option is to team up with an expert in your area who is already offering this type of program and partner with them for your wellness program.

   Realizing the financial commitment and investment to launch a program is key to your success. Many people go into this with blinders on... Financial planning provides the clarity to avoid unnecessary stress.

3. **Create Marketing Material to Launch the Wellness Program**

   Now it's time to create all the marketing material to launch the program properly. A wellness program campaign is essential for a successful launch. Create a variety of marketing materials to reach your audience and inform them of your program.

   Your campaign can include the following marketing mix: posters, team buttons, flyers, postcards, email blast, promotion, announcement in your newsletter, website update, maybe t-shirt, press release, etc. Don't count on only an email blast to get the word out. That's not going to provide the results you need. If you develop the right marketing campaign, your program will produce revenue from the very beginning and be a big success! Marketing is a huge factor to whether your program will succeed or fail.

4. **Managing the Program**
   Having systems and a structure to manage the program is the only way to deliver consistency and ensure growth. Make sure all program steps are well thought out and detailed, from scheduling the treatment, to the experience itself, to the tools to perform the wellness program, to the software program to track progress, etc. A good idea is to do a soft launch first. Offer a complimentary experience to loyal clients prior to your launch date to ensure a smooth delivery.

5. **Measuring Results**
   Whenever you launch a new program, there have to be performance measures. There are several things to measure:
   a. How Effective is Your Marketing Campaign
   b. How Many New Programs Have You Sold – Actual vs. Budget
   c. Guest Satisfaction
   d. ROI – Return On Investment
   e. Team Skills

   If you don't measure, you won't know what needs improvement. You must focus on performance indicators to determine if your program is a success.

6. **Team Contribution**
   For a project like this to succeed, you must have the entire team engaged. Take time to train receptionists and the rest of your team on the program and its benefits so they can

help promote it. Cross marketing within the medi/spa is one of the least expensive marketing tools; your team can easily recommend your wellness program to their clients if they are educated on it.

The key factor is not to try to launch too many wellness programs at one time. Take baby steps when transitioning from a day spa to a medi/wellness spa. You will find the transition much smoother and more effective.

Four Steps to Transform your Boutique into a Profit Center

The right retail mix and creative merchandising equal success! Have you assessed your Boutique's performance lately? Is it as profitable as it could be or are your products collecting dust on the shelves? It seems that most medi/spa entrepreneurs focus most of their attention on treatment revenue and pay less attention to their boutique, even though the profit margin from retail is much greater than the one from treatments. This action is causing major revenue loss.

As an industry we are not capturing our share of the personal care market. According to an SRI International & Global Summit study, beauty and anti-aging is a $679 billion industry and medi/spas are barely capturing a sliver of this market. How can you gain market shares? By focusing on the following four steps:

1. Retail Mix Selection
2. Creative Merchandising
3. Team Training
4. Performance Measures

1. Retail Mix
One of the biggest mistakes I see often is the lack of variety in retail mix within medi/spa boutiques. Most medi/spas get stuck on skincare, hair, and maybe nail products. Instead of expanding to other retail items, they expand on skincare products and carry way too many skincare brands. As a rule of thumb it's wise to have one primary and one secondary skincare line and free up your inventory budget to buy other

retail items, helping the guests to continue their medi/spa experience at home.

Attend gift shows and select de-stress products such as music, aromatherapy, books, neck wraps, etc. – products your target market would like to have. In addition, I am a big fan of branded items; I love selling or giving away t-shirts, stress balls, hats, or caps as a gift with purchase. This action will turn all your clients into medi/spa promoters, and I don't see enough medi/spas practicing this.

The other important factor is to select products at the right price and make sure you manage your inventory, order just the right quantities for your sales cycles, and manage your cash flow.

2. **Creative Merchandising**

   Merchandising is a fun function if you let the creativity flow, but often I just see the products lined up on the shelves like little soldiers, one after another. This tactic does not entice or pique your guests' interest. You would multiply your product sales if you added points of interest and tell a story on the shelf.

   You can tell stories by using some of the ingredients in the products, shelf talkers, electronic frames, elevation, sampling opportunities, and so on. You could also feature your professional treatments and the home care products that complement the treatments.

   It's also wise to keep moving inventory in order to keep your merchandise fresh and give the impression that you have new items in your boutique.

   90% of communication is non-verbal and color plays an important role in the sales process as it evokes emotional response. Use color to capture attention; paint an accent wall. Use appropriate lighting to highlight certain areas featuring the product of the month or a special promotion you are offering.

Merchandising should engage your clients and take them on a sensory experience; when you do that you increase sales. Merchandising should focus on the benefits your clients will gain and compel them to purchase your products again and again.

3. **Team Training**

Who on your team is trained to manage the boutique and ensure its success? Your team should be trained on merchandising, inventory management, and sales; are they? The number one killer in retail is the phrase, "May I help you?"

How often do you walk into a store, still hear that phrase, and automatically reply, "No thanks?" Yet sales associates, medi/spa receptionists, and other retail clerks still ask this silly question. This question should be buried, never to surface again. For a team to succeed in engaging the guests and generate sales, they need training; no one is born a sales expert. Just like in sports no one is going to win an Olympic Medal if they don't spend hours and years practicing over and over. Yet in the medi/spa industry we expect to be successful by skipping sales training. Companies cannot survive if they think sales is a dirty little word. If you want to be successful at anything, training is a requirement.

To be successful in retail, your team must be able to effectively communicate with your guests. Guests buy products when they trust, like, and see value in what is being presented to them. They buy when they see that your products are going to solve a problem. They buy when your team members come across as professionals and experts.

Spend time training your team how to approach the guest and how to make recommendations and see your sales soar.

4. **Measuring Performance**

During the Leap Ahead Medi/Spa Leader seminar, I ask attendees several questions: What is your boutique's revenue per square foot? What is your boutique's turnover rate? How much are your sales by transaction or by receptionist? Often, I don't get an answer or I get a guestimate. If you are serious about your business, you need to know these answers. Measuring your performance is the only way to improve. Here are some retail concepts and formulas to help you determine how well your boutique is performing.

Revenue per Square Foot

This is an important concept and how retailers measure their performance, and so should you.

Total Net Sales ÷ Square Feet of Selling Space = Sales per Square Foot

Example: $400,000 in revenue ÷ 800 Sq. Ft = $500 per square foot.

Turnover Rate

This refers to how often you turnover your inventory. A good turnover rate is 4 to 5.

Calculating turnover

Annual Retail Sales ÷ Average Inventory at the Beginning of the Month for Each Month of the Previous Year = Turnover

Let's assume your inventory is $10,000 each month x 12 = average inventory of $120,000 for the year. If sales were $600,000 what would the turnover be?

$600,000 divided by $120,000 = 5, a very good turnover rate.

Sales per Transaction

This measures how much you are averaging per guest. We also call it Retail Volume per Guest.
Gross Sales ÷ Number of Transactions = Sales per Transaction
Or Retail Volume ÷ Receptionist = Sales by Receptionist

Measure your performance and see how well you are doing. If you are doing well, congratulations! If not, develop retail and merchandising strategies and begin implementing new retail concepts. If you don't have time to develop your strategies, reach out to professional companies to assist you. No need to reinvent the wheel.

The important fact to remember is that you have a golden opportunity within your facility to generate a large amount of revenue and experience exponential growth. Focus on your boutique and practice the four steps I shared with you and you will elevate your success.

Your Relaxation Lounge Experience

I was staying in a five-star resort last weekend and decided to go to the medi/spa for a body treatment. The body treatment was a pleasure for me this time! It was a very nice place, so I had high expectations. I checked in, changed, and got to the relaxation lounge only to be disappointed. I was expecting a nice selection of healthy snacks and drinks only to find tea and dried pineapples. "What's up with that?" I thought to myself.

Frankly, I was surprised. I was paying $210 for a body treatment and being served dried pineapples? Your day spa down the street has a better selection of spa refreshments than that. So this experience got me thinking about the saying, "A way to a man's heart is through his stomach." Well, so is the way to a great medi/spa experience!

I don't know about you, but being cheap with your refreshment bar is not the way to a high guest retention rate. Remember, you need to focus on the *entire* experience, from the phone call and the check-in to the relaxation lounge and the treatment, etc. It's the overall experience that's important, especially when the price of one treatment is over two hundred dollars! The higher your price is, the better your relaxation lounge experience needs be.

I have a client who owns two day spas and when you go to her relaxation lounge, you are given a menu to choose a flavored smoothie, a fruit kabob, a choice of nuts, and other beverages. You literally *feel* the hospitality. By offering this extra value, she kills her competition! People love going to her spas because she takes good care of them.

So, I ask you, what is your relaxation lounge experience like?

While we are talking about the relaxation lounge, let me share another thing that drives me crazy: the way the furniture is usually positioned. For some reason, people are stuck about lining up furniture along walls instead of creating cozy and warm environments. I was in a medi/spa that had reclining chairs, but when I reclined, they had spotlights shining right into my eyes! This was another five star property. It just goes to show that the medi/spa team members who work in this particular medi/spa have not sat in their chairs to experience what their guests do. If someone had, they would either change the lighting, install dimmers, or reposition the lights to avoid blinding their guests, or simply reposition the chairs.

The other thing that bothers me is reading materials that are typically found in the relaxation lounge. Specifically, magazines that advertise over the counter products from Lancome and Estee Lauder, etc. Here we are trying to convince them to buy *our* products, yet we are refreshing our guests' minds with over the counter brands right before they go for their treatment! Help me understand this logic... Wouldn't it be better to have books on health, wellness, beauty, and fitness; things you stand for and believe in?

Or how about the medi/spas that have a TV in the relaxation lounge? This one kills me. If you are going to have a TV, it better be playing your medi/spa channel promoting all your products and services, showing before and after photos, sharing wellness tips, and so on. Since I am on a roll here, here's one more thing that drives me crazy! It's when we serve things in the lounge that we don't sell. From tea to neck wraps, every product you use, make sure you sell it, too!

How about this scenario: I've been in relaxation lounges where you sit with a drink and there is no place to put it down between sips. I can go on and on... My advice to you is to experience your own relaxation lounge. Go through your guest experience steps yourself to see how friendly your medi/spa environment is and what you need to change.

Remember, it's about presentation and retention. Impress guests with your hospitality so they will remember your experience and love it so much that they want to come back over and over!

So take a look at your relaxation lounge budget. Make the necessary adjustments to enhance your guest experience offerings and watch your guest retention rate and reservations increase! How would you rate your relaxation lounge experience?

Dori Recommends....

To help you with your business you can tap into the following effective tools:

Sign up for a secret shopping and On-Site Assessment and discover ways to improve your business!

Experience Oops and Retention Rate

While visiting my friend one summer, we decided to go and get pedicures. We called a new day spa near her house, made an appointment, and off we went. When Gerri and I checked in, we met our nail techs and were escorted to a very nice pedicure area. So far, so good! We sat back, got settled, and the experience began.

We soaked our feet for few minutes, then were asked to take them out of the water. They dried them and then proceeded to apply a thick, white, gel-like substance to the bottom of our heels. Then they placed gauze on top of it and proceeded to work on our toes.

One thing I don't like about getting pedicures is toenail filing. I often wonder if the nail techs ever had a pedicure themselves, because who would file such small nails with such force? It feels terrible, doesn't it? So I informed my nail tech that I prefer she cuts my toenails and to please perform very light filing. That went well and I was happy.

Before I continue with the story, I have to tell you that Gerri and I take very good care of our feet. We don't have callous problems and receive pedicures on a regular basis. We may have a little dryness, but that is it. Once they were done with the toes, they took a callous remover scrubber, took off the gauze from our heels and began the scrub the bottom of our feet. This is when I was shocked! I saw layers of my heel falling down. It's as if they took a knife and cut the bottom of my heel off. I knew then and there this was not good. Gerri and I were looking at each other wondering what kind of product that was. Remember, neither one of us had callouses to remove. I knew this was not going got be a good thing. So I asked the nail tech, "What was that?" She said it was callous remover. I thought to myself, "No, it's more like heel remover." So they finished our pedicures and we left.

Days later, Gerri and I were talking on the phone. We both noticed that our heels were growing thicker and harder. We were both concerned. We were so proud of our heels before the pedicure and now we have a hard formation where the nail techs carved our skin like you carve a turkey.

So I am asking, have you ever had this type of experience? Why did the nail techs use this product when it was not needed? Do you believe that if you remove the skin on the heel it will come back harder? And as an industry, how can we avoid mistakes like this? You know we will never go back to that place!

Medi/Spas wonder why their retention rate is not as high as it should be, and this is why! Things like this happen all the time. Guests visit your medi/spa, but if their experience was not customized according to *their* needs, they won't come back! Not everyone needs the same products and the same protocols. Not everyone has the same issues. Maybe this product works great on some people who have issues with callouses, but it certainly was not the right product or treatment for us. They could have gained my friend as a regular client, but they won't now!

Let's talk about retention rate and how we can improve it. Do you track your retention rate? Do you call people who have visited your medi/spa but have not returned to see why they haven't been back? If you don't want to call, at least send an electronic survey to see why they haven't returned.

Remember: If you don't know what's wrong, you can't fix it!

Dori Recommends….

To help you with your business you can tap into the following effective tools:

Therapist Manual and Training.
Train the team on treatment protocols that everyone must follow.

Ensuring Medi/Spa Profits During Holidays

You know the old saying, "If you fail to plan, you are planning to fail?" Don't postpone your success! Here are eight tips to help you celebrate next holiday season.

Eight Steps You Need to Take
1. Merchandising Mix
2. Gift Card Packages
3. Decorating the Medi/Spa
4. Holiday Event
5. E-news Marketing
6. Special Client Gifts
7. Team Targets
8. Team Party

1. Merchandising Mix
Decide what new gift items you want to offer and order them in October. Create a festive way to package them. Bundling a few medi/spa items together is a good idea, but make sure the packaging is attractive and irresistible. You want low, medium, and high price points in order to appeal to different clientele. Run reports to determine what sold very well for you last year and do something similar. Don't get stocked up on only skin care. Combine skin care with other items like CD's, bath products, accessories, candles, books, etc. Get creative and involve your team in the process. If they are sold on the items, your team is more likely to promote and sell them.

2. Gift Card Packages
Gift card sales are always a big hit during the holidays, but here is a tip on how to maximize your gift card sales. Don't sell gift cards alone. Create three to four packages of gift cards and include product gifts within each one. So instead

of someone just buying a gift card, they are able to buy a gift with the card. Create a flyer featuring three or four packages and make sure they are at different price points. Display the gifts in a prominent area within the medi/spa to attract attention and make people aware of the packages. This really works! You can increase your gift card sales tremendously.

3. Decorating the Medi/Spa
Make the medi/spa ambiance festive, but keep it simple. Remember, less is more. Include your products within the decorations. A simple thing to do is to display beautifully wrapped packages with ribbons, especially by the gift card area. Have fun and get creative!

4. Holiday Event
What a great way to thank all your clients and generate revenue at the same time! Planning a holiday party should involve the whole team.

5. E-news Marketing
Prepare and send out gift card promotions via email. Inform your clients of all the fun and exciting things you have going on this season. Include some medi/spa cuisine recipes and tips on how to stay healthy during the holiday season, and of course promote your gift packages. If you don't have an e-newsletter, check out Ready-to-Go E-news from InSPAration Management.

6. Special Client Gifts
We all have special clients that spend a lot of money. You want to show your appreciation to them with some sort of gift. Let them know they are special to you!

7. Team Targets

Set team targets for service, retail, and gift card package sales. Make a contest and give the winners or whoever reaches the target something special. Get the team excited about the opportunities they have.

8. Team Party

A team appreciation party is a must! Do something special to let them know how valued they are!

Go ahead and get started. We found the best way to get these things done is to schedule them into your calendar and begin working on them. If you start early and don't procrastinate, you and your team will have a great holiday season.

Dori Recommends….

To help you with your business you can tap into the following effective tools:

Secrets to Successful Event Planning USB

Four Ways to Maximize Your Retail Revenue

When was the last time you went to a medi/spa and had an experience where the therapist actually talked to you about adding a treatment to what you already selected from the menu? Or when was the last time a therapist actually recommended a product to use at home? You probably don't remember or it rarely happens. Actually, the fact is most guests leave medi/spas empty-handed... except for cruise spas.

You are probably a medi/spa professional reading this and also a medi/spa goer, as we all go to medi/spas. In my position as a consultant and coach, I have visited medi/spas around the world, have been a secret shopper for many medi/spas, and rarely do people recommend to me. Normally you go into a treatment room, they tell you to lie down, begin the treatment, and when you are finished, they let you go empty-handed. This practice is costing medi/spa leaders millions of dollars.

On the other hand, I took my family on a cruise and, of course, I visited the medi/spa several times during the trip. What a difference in their entire approach! They take the time to discover your needs, then recommend treatments and products. The amazing thing is they do it consistently! I know this is the protocol on most cruise ships as I experience the same type of service on other cruise lines. If the team on a cruise ship can do it, why can't resort spas, day spas, and medi-spas do it, too?

InSPAration Management has conducted many studies on retail and treatment upgrades. We found that they are two of the biggest missed revenue opportunities within a medi/spa. Many medi/spas focus on delivering a great treatment experience, but totally ignore additional treatment suggestions and retail recommendations for home. As an industry, we are missing out on significant revenue that can be generated through both of these revenue streams. It's a fact: billions of dollars are spent on beauty and self-care products per year! Unfortunately, most medi/spas don't get their market share. Thousands of dollars are left on the table, leading to slimmer profit lines.

Daily, we hear from medi/spa leaders who are frustrated with the lack of retail sales and upgrade opportunities. When we ask, "What are the repercussions for lack of sales?" normally there are none. How can you expect to improve performance and achieve new results if the team is not held accountable for their actions? If you want to begin tapping into these missed revenue opportunities, you must implement the following four steps in order for your team to produce the results you desire.

1. Set Medi/Spa Performance Expectations and Measures
2. Tie Compensation to Performance
3. Implement a Recommending System
4. Train and Coach the Team

1. Set Medi/Spa Performance Expectations and Measures

You get what you expect and what you measure. To improve medi/spa performance, you must set expectations. What does it mean to be a professional therapist on your team?

What are their professional obligations? You will need to outline them in detail. Set targets for both treatment volume and retail volume per guest. Then measure often. Don't wait until the end of the month to realize they did not hit the target; it's too late then. Just like in sports, the goal is to get to the playoffs, then win the championship. In order to do that, the coach tracks statistics from *every single game*. You need to do the same. Track performance daily and watch your profit line grow!

2. Tie Compensation to Performance

Tying compensation to performance is essential. If a team member is not recommending, they don't deserve to earn the same amount of money as the one who does. Tying service commission to retail commission is a sure way to make the team recommend more. That is why the cruise ships do so well in retail. Their compensation plan rewards retail sales. Does yours? Compensation plays a big role and it must be addressed if you want to improve performance.

3. Develop a Recommending System

To succeed you must have a recommending system. Systems insure consistency, accuracy, and growth. Without a proven and effective system, your future is uncertain. Fortunately, there are systems available to help you. We teach the PRIDE Recommending System. It's called, "Don't Sell, Recommend!" It's a philosophy focused on delivering a complete guest experience in the medi/spa *and* at home. The system identifies guests' needs or concerns while making recommendations using the PRIDE System.

4. Training and Coaching the Team

Training and coaching is a never-ending process. Someone must be responsible for training and coaching the team. Who is the coach in your organization? Training is an essential component to your success. It needs to be conducted often and must include role playing. Just like in sports again, the team listens to the coach, then they go out on the floor to practice what they learned. That's role play... but in our industry, the therapists say, "I hate to role play." Many medi/spa leaders accept that reply and don't role play. Can you imagine a basketball or a soccer player telling his coach I don't want to role play? How long will that player be on a winning team? You get my point... they must role play. The more they do it, the more comfort and confidence they will have with the entire recommending process.

It's time for the medi/spa industry to realize the opportunities they have and start recommending as a way of life. Focus on these four strategies, set new guest experience standards for your medi/spa, and maximize your revenue generation. Need help? Seek out an educational firm to guide you and implement proven, effective systems. Work smarter, not harder to maximize your success!

Dori Recommends....

To help you with your business you can tap into the following effective tools:

**Recipes For Success
CoachMe Series**

**Don't Sell, Recommend!
USB**

Chapter 3:

Your Financial Health

"The number one problem in today's generation and economy is the lack of financial literacy."
- Alan Greenspan

Budgeting for Success

In working with many clients, often I hear that they don't have a detailed budget. Do you have a budget? Do you know your financial ratios?

Lately, I have been receiving some scary phone calls from medi/spa owners seeking help. These calls represent all shapes and sizes of the medi/spa industry, from large multi-million dollar businesses to solo-preneurs, and the topic of the conversations is, "I am not making any profits," "I am not making enough profit," or, "I am working so hard and at the end of the year I have nothing to show for it." And in some cases they are in the red, big time. I like the color red, but not on a financial statement. I much prefer black. Don't you?

There is a saying in business, "Cash is king!" Although, when you don't have cash at the end of the month, it's an indication of three factors:

1. Your financial ratios are out of whack
2. You are spending beyond your means
3. You're not generating revenue due to lack of marketing

You've heard me talk about financial ratios before. As a matter of fact, we have a couple of free webinars on www.InSPArationManagement.com that you can view to help you further understand your finances.

You must conduct a financial ratio analysis for your business. There are three financial terms you need to be very familiar with:

1. Liquidity: Your ability to pay short-term debts and obligations on time.

2. Debt: Amount of money needed to run your day to day business.

3. Profitability: The amount of money you take to the bank after paying all your expenses.

The one mistake I see over and over that affects your profit line is the compensation model and payroll cost. Many medi/spa owners are not making any profits due to lack of tying compensation to performance. If you want to pay someone the outrageous rates you are paying, then you need to at least have them earn it.

You will not make any profits if your operating costs and your payroll costs are too high. Owners are hesitant to change their compensation model due to the fear that their team might leave. I totally understand that, but what is the alternative?

• Working for free
• Going out business
• Not sleeping at night
• Getting sick because of stress

Or you can keep the same team and regret being in business and/or lose your passion for why you started your business in the first place. The choice is yours. Something has to change. Go on a recruiting mission. There are many people who are looking for jobs. I know it's difficult to make changes, but if you don't make the change, you will keep getting the same results and stay broke.

However, here is the brightest idea! If you have an effective marketing plan and you are keeping your team busy, they will make money without you paying huge commissions.

You see, 50% of nothing is nothing. For example, Massage Envy is the fastest growing franchise and they only pay their team $15 per hour when they are working, plus tips, in most cases. They employ thousands of massage therapists and estheticians, and everyone is making money. Why? Because they are busy! So you see, it's not about the commission rate, it's about how busy they are and how much money they can earn!

The bright idea here is to assess your compensation model as soon as possible and make necessary adjustments so you can achieve a healthy business. Determine your budget and develop a healthy business!

Dori Recommends....

To help you with your business you can tap into the following effective tools:

VPG Compensation Model USB

Medi/Spa Budget USB

Business Financial Health

When business owners first go into business they are excited, eager, motivated, and can't wait to get started. Then reality sets in and the bills start piling up, followed by pressure, tension, and anxiety. If you are like most owners, you are always looking for ways to cut expenses and generate more revenue so it's worth it to be in business.

The main reason entrepreneurs go into business for themselves is to be their own boss, have more freedom, and make more money. But here is the sad fact: in most cases business owners don't pay themselves; they end up working harder and make less money. According to US census statistics, an average business makes about 7% net profit. Yes, there are some businesses that make more, some less, and some make none. Where do you stand? Are your overhead expenses diminishing your bottom line? If so, read on and discover four strategies to gain financial health.

1. **Have a Budget**
   Most medi/spa owners who call our office seeking business help don't have a budget. Without a budget, you are allowing your business to manage you instead of you managing it. Whether you have a large, medium, small, or even a solo-preneur business, you must have a budget. Your budget should include a monthly breakdown of all your finances, such as:

   - Number of clients you expect to see monthly
   - Forecasted service revenue
   - Forecasted retail revenue

- Product cost
- Compensation cost
- Operating cost
- Marketing expenses
- Budgeted profit

The key is to detail the budget as much as possible so your revenue goals are clear and to be disciplined enough to not overspend.

2. **Your P & L Statement**
   The profit and loss statement is your monthly report card. This allows you to see your financial ratios and ensure they are aligned. There are four important financial ratios to measure.

   i. Operating Expenses
   ii. Product Cost
   iii. Compensation Cost
   iv. Profits

   Operating expenses and compensation are the biggest two expenses for a business. In most cases we find that the compensation ratio is too high. To be profitable, your compensation ratio cannot exceed 40% of your overall budget. For example, of each dollar that comes into your business you can afford to pay $0.40 towards compensation. If your compensation cost is more than that then you are at risk of having an unhealthy business.

3. **Managing Your Inventory**
   Inventory is a big expense if it's not managed properly. Your inventory includes your retail, your professional products,

guest supplies, team supplies, etc. Use your software system to track your inventory and manage your retail and professional turnover rate. We often find overuse of professional products and that the team is upgrading treatments and not charging the guest for it. That will cause the treatment cost to go up and diminish your profits. To prevent this from happening, we recommend having a dispensary and pre-measuring products used to have better professional cost control.

As for retail, you must have self-discipline and not overspend. You must calculate your "open to buy" rate to avoid overspending.

4. Expense Management Tips

Guest Supplies
- ✓ Avoid using paper goods such as cups and plates. Use glass instead or washable, durable high-end plastic. This will represent a big savings over time.
- ✓ To save on laundry, only offer robes to guests who are having multiple treatments.
- ✓ Use paper for waxing clients. This will save on wear and tear of your linen and laundry.
- ✓ Control the team's intake of the refreshments. This can get very expensive if you are supplying the team with snacks and gourmet drinks.

Paper Copies
Place PDF files of all your client files online and recommend they go to your website to download their forms, print, complete, and bring back with them. This will save you a

large amount of paper and ink as well as time. Or they can complete them online and email them to you.

Suppliers' Contributions

Your suppliers can contribute to your event, samples, and training. Make sure you set up a meeting to discuss their contribution to help you cut expenses. Sampling can be very costly without the vendor's contribution, and to sell you must be able to sample products.

Gratuity Processing Fees

This is a cost that many medi/spa owners do not take into account. When a guest gives the gratuity on a credit card, the medi/spa owner pays a credit card processing fee on that transaction, therefore increasing your cost. Some medi/spas are enforcing cash only tips. Or you can charge your team a processing fee out of the gratuity prior to paying them in order to avoid this additional payroll cost.

Bartering to Cut Cost

You can barter many services to cut cost. For example, your bookkeeping and accounting cost can be bartered, your fresh flowers, refreshments, graphic design, website updates, almost everything can be bartered. That automatically provides you cost reduction. We encourage you to build bartering relations and become more profitable.

The medi/spa industry is filled with right-brained professionals who are more artistic and who don't care very much for numbers. But if you want to be a successful businessperson, you need to fall in love with numbers and look at them often to measure your success. This is your path to having a financially healthy business!

Dori Recommends….

To help you with your business you can tap into the following effective tools:

Visit InSPArationManagement.com and take a Financial Assessment.

Managing Your Medi/Spa Team's Gratuity

Tips to help you recoup some of your expenses

Medi/spa profits are already slim, but when you start adding all the gratuity credit card processing fees, they get even slimmer. Have you calculated how much your team's gratuity credit card processing fees are costing you?

Well, it is time you did. This amount adds up to thousands of dollars per year, and it's all coming out of your pocket! Most medi/spa owners don't take that into account when creating a compensation model.

What you need to do:
1. Calculate how much you pay on average for processing gratuity on credit card. What rate are you paying on average?
2. Share the situation with your team.
3. Present them with the following options:

Option A. You can stop accepting gratuity on credit cards. If the client wants to give a gratuity, it can only be in cash. (This option is not good from the guests' standpoint or from the therapists' stand point). Many people do not carry cash; therefore, therapists may not receive a gratuity and guests will leave feeling bad.

Option B. Continue accepting gratuity on credit cards, but pass on the cost of the processing fee to the therapists. Begin withdrawing the credit card processing fee of 5% from the gratuity payout. This is the best option.

Option "B" is a win-win situation.

This will help you cut back on expenses as a business owner and align the therapists' compensation payout some.

Another point worth mentioning is when to pay out the gratuity. In working with one of our clients, I discovered that she settles the gratuity payout on a daily basis. Many times, this causes her to pay out cash from her own pocket! Are you doing that? If so, you need to stop *now*!

A daily gratuity payout process presents two problems:

1. As a business owner, you should not have to reach into your own pocket for cash, especially when the gratuity was placed on a credit card. This is a double negative for you.

2. Therapists end up spending their gratuity rather than saving it or seeing it as a significant part of their compensation.

Best practice: Gratuity left on credit cards should be paid with the regular payroll. Indicate the amount of gratuity on a separate line, deduct your credit card processing fee, and pay it with the commission payroll.

We found that this method helps therapists save their money and have a better handle on their finances. It's also good for the business owner because it reduces the amount of accounting you need to do and simplifies the entire credit card gratuity process.

We have implemented this method in many medi/spas and it works great! Try it. We hope you find it helpful.

Team Compensation

Are you still paying your medi/spa team the same old way and getting the same mediocre results? Switch to a performance based compensation model and watch your business grow!

Remember how happy you were when you first decided to go into business for yourself and act upon your entrepreneurial spirit? You had big dreams and a vivid vision of how your medi/spa was going to be, delivering great guest experiences while operating a successful, profitable business. Are you living your dream? Or is the pressure of running and sustaining your business clouding your dream? Whatever ambition drove you to open or operate a medi/spa, an important factor for your business is profitability. Is your medi/spa as profitable as it can be?

There are two significant challenges facing medi/spa leaders and operators:
1. High compensation rates
2. Low profit margin

Many medi/spa operators are caught in the status quo. For decades, most medi/spa compensation plans pay between 40% to 65% commission on services. This structure has many pitfalls and should be replaced with a motivational compensation plan based on targets and performance such as the VPG ComPlan.

What is the VPG ComPlan?
VPG stands for Volume per Guest. As a medi/spa operator, VPG is a valuable financial tool used for measuring medi/spa performance and profitability. VPG reveals the average revenue generated per guest. It's one of the most important financial concepts.

Volume per Guest Formula
VPG = Service Volume/Number of Guests
Service VPG
Susie's service volume for the month is $7,000
She serviced 70 guests
Her service Volume per Guest is $100
Retail VPG
Susie's retail volume for the month is $1,000
She serviced 70 guests
Her retail VPG is $14.29

Go ahead and calculate your VPG.
Calculate each therapist's VPG for service and retail to discover where you stand.

In Bradford D. Smart's book *Top Grading*, he outlines the importance of discovering who is on your team based on job performance. Every organization has A, B, C, and some D players. When creating a compensation plan, it is important to pay the A players what they are worth. As performance delivery increases, so should the compensation. Why pay everyone equally if performance is not equal?

The VPG compensation plan is based on the Volume per Guest ratio and an escalated commission scale, or it could also be an hourly rate depending on your structure.

VPG Compensation Model
The first step is to set a VPG target for your medi/spa. Let's assume your medi/spa's target is to reach and exceed $100.00 VPG. Your medi/spa's VPG target needs to be understood by therapists, incorporating it into their own personal target. The VPG commission structure is based on the medi/spa's VPG target. Commission will vary depending on whether therapists reach their target or not. *The structure is based purely on performance.* When a therapist

reaches the VPG target, a high commission is earned. If the VPG target is not achieved, less commission is paid out.

VPG ComPlan Model Benefits

- Provide targets and goals to focus on and strive towards
- Encourage upgrade opportunities, resulting in increased service VPG
- Increase retail VPG
- Promote performance, stretching to reach the highest target
- Reward exceptional performance
- Reduce payroll cost
- Performance awareness to medi/spa leadership and team
- Foster a motivational environment
- Create a great management and recruiting tool

Compensation Reflection in Overall Budget

Prior to developing your compensation model, it is essential to determine your budget ratios including all the compensation mix components you offer. Adjust the commission scale to meet your desired ratios. The Overall Budget Ratios chart is a sample ratio model.

Mistakes to Avoid

1. Not counting gratuity as part of the compensation mix.

Normally, people in the service industry earn a very small salary or hourly rate with a large portion of their income based on gratuity. In the medi/spa industry, extremely high commissions are paid on services (anywhere from 40 to 65%) while also allowing therapists to make an additional 15% to 20% in gratuity! Take a waiter or waitress for example, they earn minimum wage plus their gratuity. Restaurants do not pay server employees 50% for the all the tables they served + salary + gratuity. Why is it that the medi/spa industry does? This is the reason so many medi/spas suffer from profit-itis.

Show gratuity as part of the entire income opportunity you offer your employees and elevate your profit margin!

2. Key Performance Indicators

KPI are other performance measurements that are important to you, such as:

- Retention
- Professionalism
- Image
- Skills
- Teamwork

KPI can be part of your monthly bonus and part of your compensation mix.

3. Avoid a compensation model that is not based on targets.

If you are still operating your business without targets, you deserve what you are getting. Wake up and smell the roses! Start holding your team accountable for their performance.

4. Unawareness of your overall compensation plan pay out.

If you are still operating your medi/spa without a detailed budget, you won't be able to grow your business and you won't know your ComPlan payout ratio to the overall budget.

Need help with you budget? Purchase the budget template.

It's essential to offer a compensation plan that attracts and retains professional individuals. Retaining employees and investing in them is less costly than operating with a high employee turnover rate. Creating the right compensation plan will produce a motivated, professional medi/spa team. It increases profitability while enhancing guest experiences and employee satisfaction.

Dori Recommends....

To help you with your business you can tap into the following effective tools:

Experience Fresh Start. We help you launch a new compensation model and we train your team to be more productive. Visit InSPArationManagement.com for more information.

The Million-Dollar Question: What Should My Profit Margin Be?

I was listening to one of the ISPA audio lectures the other day and the speaker was saying how her spa was generating over 40% in profit for the past few years. That's a good margin if you have a resort spa. I can just imagine the faces of all the medi/spa owners in the room thinking to themselves, "I don't even have double digit profit… how is 40% profit possible?"

Myth and reality: profit margins vary tremendously. It depends on which business model you have. It's different for resort, medi, and day spas.

In resort spas, the spa normally has no major expenses. The hotel or resort operates the spa and it is not a standalone business in most cases. Therefore, the spa does not pay rent, laundry, electricity, maintenance, etc. The main cost the resort spa has is product cost and human capital payroll. The reality is: it's easy to earn 40% in profit when you don't have to pay for major operating expenses!

Medi-spas connected to a dermatology center or operated by plastic surgeons are in a similar situation as with resorts. Again, in most cases, the practice pays the bills. So profit margin should be around 40% to 50%.

Medi-spas and day spas that operate as stand-alone businesses are responsible for all operational expenses, compensation, product cost, and marketing. Therefore, the profit margin is significantly smaller. Depending on your medi/spa's operating expenses, payroll rate, and overhead, an acceptable profit margin is 10% to 15%.

The other main differential is medi/spa marketing. With most resort spas and medi-spas, clients are on location already; all you have to do is motivate them to come into the medi/spa. Stand-alone medi/spas have a broader challenge. They have to be very creative in driving traffic into their medi/spa and generally have larger marketing expenses.

The medi/spa business model is the most challenging. The biggest challenge facing medi/spa owners is compensation rate. This is the number one concern we hear about all the time. Most medi/spas are running 50% and higher compensation rates, leading to minimal profits.

Reality check: If you operate a stand-alone medi/spa business, it's time for a financial check-up. You need to identify your financial ratios and set a goal to trim your compensation while increasing capacity and volume in order to improve your profit margin.

Do you know your financial ratios? To know your ratios, you need a budget to use as a financial blueprint to guide you. Contact us; we can help!

Chapter 4:
Medi/Spa Team Motivation & Implementation

"People often say that motivation doesn't last. Well, neither does bathing - that's why we recommend it daily."

- Zig Ziglar

Positioning New Employees for Success!

You just hired a new team member. Now what? As a medi/spa leader, it's your responsibility to position your new employee for success. That takes time, effort, and business tools. In this section, you will discover three essential training steps to prepare your new employee for success so they can deliver a great guest experience, generate revenue, and maximize their effectiveness.

To position your team and your medi/spa for success, a leader must have training manuals and implement the following three steps to train new employees.

Step One: Orientation Training

In the corporate world, most new employees attend at least a one-day company orientation. This training is designed to introduce the company's operating guidelines and relationship expectations. In the medi/spa industry, I mostly see company orientation happening in resort spas. Most medi-spas and day spas skip this important training. Their orientation (in most cases) consists of job shadowing with an existing employee. There is no system in place or an orientation manual, or even an employee handbook to train new employees. This practice is a recipe for failure. It does not set a successful foundation, nor does it make a great impression about your company.

Successful companies have two important manuals:
A. An Orientation Booklet
B. An Employee Manual

These documents establish your professionalism and show new employees that you mean business. Working for your company is not a game. You have structure, systems, values, and a clear vision that are important to you as a leader and crucial for your team to follow and practice.

A. The orientation booklet should describe your operating guidelines, policies, procedures, dress code, behavioral expectations, guest experience protocols, training curriculum schedule, and other dos and don'ts. New employees should have a clear picture and understanding of expectations after reading your orientation booklet.

B. Your employee manual should offer clarity on topics such as paid time off, harassment policies, employment policies, confidentiality, non-compete, compensation, and other essential employee guidelines. The employee manual is important for two reasons:

1. To protect your business.
2. To provide your team with a reference tool.

The employee handbook and orientation booklet are essential to your company. They provide a good foundation for new employees, allowing medi/spa leaders to properly manage, avoid ambiguity, and minimize misunderstandings.

These two booklets can be separate or combined. Upon completion of this training, new employees sign off that they received it, read it, and agree to operate by company guidelines.

Orientation should be conducted on the first day of work for the new hire and take a few hours to cover all the material. It is important to have new employees sign that they have received their handbooks. This will help you increase your employment retention rate and give the employee clarity as to what it means to be on your team and work within your organization.

Step Two: Technical Training
For new therapists to deliver a great guest experience and ensure your guests' satisfaction, it is essential to train them on all your menu items and upgrade opportunities you offer your clients. Keep in mind that no matter how experienced your new employees are, they must go through your technical training!

In some cases, the brands you carry may send *their* trainer to train new employees. If not, your department lead or whoever is qualified to train *must train them*. Training should include your unique rituals, procedures, use of professional products, equipment, cleanliness, sanitation, retail range, pricing, etc.

Technical training could take two days or more depending on how many treatments and products you have. The main thing to keep in mind is not to shortcut training. Shortcutting leads to guest attrition and a lack of consistency in your business.

Having a technical manual from your supplier is great but not enough. As a leader, you must have a therapist manual for training purposes. It should outline all protocols, rituals, product usage, guest communication, etc. This will help you deliver consistent training and avoid the process of reinventing the wheel every time you hire a new person.

A good practice is to assign a buddy to your new employee until she/he is totally acclimated with all your processes, treatments, and equipment.

Step Three: Business Skills

Business skills training is missing in most medi/spas, yet it is one of the most important steps of the new hire process, team training, and professional growth.

It is not enough to train on technical knowledge alone. If you are serious about your success, you must have a business curriculum to train your team on business essentials and profitability.

Here are some of the most important topics to include within your business training manual:

A. Performance Expectation and Income Potential. Give the team clearly defined monthly goals; share the career path they can chart within your company and the income potential they can achieve if they are a high performer.

B. Train on the Guest Consultation Process and the importance of multiple treatments to assist the guest in achieving and maintaining their desired results. Tapping into series and upgrading is crucial to achieve results and satisfy your guests.

C. Home Care Recommendations via Retail. This is a major training component. Your team must understand how important it is to the guest experience, to the success of your business, and to them. Teach the recommending system and implement tools to make the process easy and beneficial for all.

D. How to Self-Promote and Cross-Market. Growth is very possible when the team learns how to self-promote and cross-market within the medi/spa. There are many easy strategies you can apply so your team is armed and prepared to increase capacity.

E. Guest Experience and Retention. Nothing is more important than retention. The cost to acquire a new client is very high and your goal as a leader is to maintain and retain them. Through business training, teach your team how to deliver great, memorable experiences to turn your guests into lifetime clients.

Of course there are many other topics to include within your business manuals and training. For now, I encourage you to get started with creating your manual and plan your training curriculum. Through training and education, everything is possible!

Dori Recommends….

To help you with your business you can tap into the following effective tools:

Visit InSPArationManagement.com and discover the team manuals.

New Belief, New Income Potential

Do you want to increase your income this year by 30% or more? You can by focusing on delivering a complete guest experience *in the medi/spa* and *at home*! The medi/spa industry does a great job with performing treatments in the medi/spa, but in most cases, misses the boat with retail opportunities and educating guests on how to take care of themselves at home *between treatments*.

Most medi/spa teams don't recognize the importance of home care products for the wellness of their clients. You mention the word products or retail and everyone panics! "You want me to sell?" The answer is, "No, you don't need to sell, you need to recommend!"

Why is selling retail such a sore subject in the medi/spa industry? Medi/Spa leaders try to maximize retail revenue to generate greater profits. Yet on the other hand, we have some team members who don't give a hoot about making home care recommendations. It seems most medi/spa teams only care about service income and don't understand how much money they are losing by not making home care recommendations.

As an industry, we are missing out on significant revenues that can be generated through retail. It's a fact that billions of dollars are spent on beauty and self-care products per year! Unfortunately, most medi/spas hardly tap into it. Thousands of dollars are left on the table because team members don't see it as part of their professional obligation and don't realize the annual income potential.

As a medi/spa professional, you have several revenue streams you can tap into. Here is an example of a typical compensation mix. In most cases, there are four potential revenue streams:

1. Service
2. Retail
3. Gratuity
 4. Benefits

Currently, you might be tapping into three of the four revenue streams while completely missing most retail revenue opportunities. How much income are you missing out on from home care retail?

Let's take a look at the compensation mix chart by revenue stream. Do you know how much revenue was generated by your compensation mix last year or last month? Do the following exercise and explore your opportunities. Let's assume this chart represents 100% of your income potential and you made $40,000 last year. You need to break down your income and see what percentage of your income ($40,000) came from services, retail, gratuity, and benefits. This exercise will help you realize additional income potential and assist you in setting new goals.

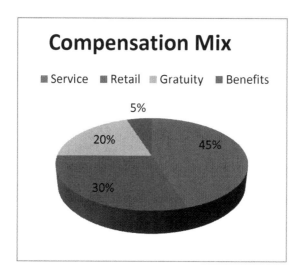

Compensation Mix

■ Service ■ Retail ■ Gratuity ■ Benefits

5%
20%
45%
30%

What can you do to maximize your income? Practice the following 12 retail commandments and experience exponential growth!

1. I will adopt a new professional philosophy: It's not about selling. It's about making professional recommendations and helping my guests.
2. I will make it a habit to discover my guests' concerns and help them; first by recommending the right treatments, then by recommending the appropriate home care.
3. I will fulfill my professional obligation by delivering a complete guest experience, both in the medi/spa and by helping my guests learn what products they need to use at home.
4. I will educate my guests on how to take care of themselves between professional treatments.
5. I understand my guests buy and use products from somewhere. Therefore, they need to buy *my* quality products instead of purchasing "over the counter" products.

6. I will use and believe in my products.
7. I will learn all about my products' ingredients so I can recommend them with confidence.
8. I will use an intake form to help discover my guests' needs and ensure their safety.
9. I will build trust and strengthen the relationship between myself and my guests.
10. I will not prejudge my guests' ability to afford my products.
11. I will set goals and strive to achieve them.
12. I will focus on recommending, not selling.

You can be like Beth with Skin Essentials in Colorado, a coaching client of InSPAration Management. She has achieved the highest volume per guest we have ever heard of. She averages $189 per guest for home care! What is your volume per guest? Here is a simple formula to calculate it. Take your retail recommending volume and divide it by the number of guests you had last month. This will determine your average volume per guest (VPG). What is your VPG?

Renew your belief system and commit to practicing the 12 commandments. There is a saying that states this simple fact, "If you help enough people get what they want, you will get what you want." I would like to stress that our number one priority is to take care of our guests. When we do, the money will follow.

Practice the "Don't Sell, Recommend" philosophy and SOAR!

Dori Recommends….

To help you with your business you can tap into the following effective tools:

Don't Sell, "Recommend"! USB

Are You Managing Your Team or Are They Managing You?

I was speaking with one of our clients last week, a spa director for a large day spa. While we were conversing she shared with me what one of her team members said to her earlier in the week. One of her estheticians was telling her, "I don't need to be selling any more retail because I sold $300 worth of products this pay period and I only made $30, so it's not worth it for me, so don't count on me doing it." And she went on telling about the tone of voice and body language that went along with it. I couldn't believe what I was hearing! I was appalled at the audacity this person had to talk to her spa director like that. You give a person a job and a great opportunity to make money and that's what you get in return.

Are you faced with this type of behavior? Do you allow your team to talk to you like that? And if they do, what do you do about it?

I was disappointed to hear the spa director tell me this story because this person (esthetician) was recently hired and all this could have been avoided if the spa director had practiced the CLARITI hiring system we teach our clients. But she did not follow the hiring steps. One main part of the hiring steps is the last "I" in CLARITI which stands for "in-writing commitment agreement." In the agreement the spa director outlines all the responsibilities, professionalism, obligations, expectations, behaviors, performance measures, and more. It includes all that is expected from a team member who is thinking about joining the medi/spa. We advise medi/spa leaders to include as many details as possible in the commitment agreement and have the person sign it. But in this case she did not, which makes managing more difficult.

See, if you discuss all these points before you hire the person and you get them to sign off on it, managing them becomes easier. Had this esthetician signed the agreement, she would have known how important retail sales are to her position and that it's her professional obligation to make recommendations to her guests and to educate them on how to take care of themselves at home, among other things.

And if she had still said that to her medi/spa director, the director could have taken her into the office and coached her on how she can make more than $30 by knowing how to recommend more products and treatments to her guests. But best of all, she could have also reminded her of the agreement that she signed and committed to.

I have two issues with this story. One is how some therapists/estheticians conduct themselves at the workplace and medi/spa directors allowing that kind of behavior at work. The sad thing is if you allow it and you don't address it, it only gets worse.

What do you do when your team talks to you like that? Share your stories with us.

Dori Recommends….

To help you with your business you can tap into the following effective tools:

**Blueprint to Effective
Team Building USB**

**Soaring Ahead
Essential Success Principles**

The Price We Pay to be the BEST

I had the pleasure of attending the All County Band performance last weekend. What a great experience! I got to watch my son, Charlie, play the tuba in the band with all his musically talented friends. We watched seventh to twelfth graders perform in three separate bands. They were the best of the best! The auditorium was packed with proud parents, friends, and school band directors from all over Central Florida to enjoy their students' hard work and excellent performances.

It was not my first time attending an All County performance. As I sat there enjoying the great music and watching the young, talented musicians, one thing stuck out: the role of the band director.

I thought, *I can't imagine the band without this person.* What would they sound like if no one was directing? Sometimes I can't turn off my business brain; I started thinking about how important this role is and how it resembles the role of a medi/spa director.

The band director is responsible for the band members and delivering a great performance or experience. Just like you! Then, I thought of all the things a band director goes through to prepare these young students to deliver a great experience for their audience. I reviewed what Charlie had to do to deliver a great performance and came up with seven steps. These steps are very similar to what your team members need to go through to deliver a great guest experience.

	Band Students	Medi/Spa Professionals
1.	Learn the music	Learn the treatments and products
2.	Practice the music	Practice the delivery
3.	Be a good listener & follow leader direction	Follow protocols and manager direction
4.	Play his part	Perform their part
5.	Practice – role play	Practice – role play
6.	Be a good tuba section team player	Be a good team player
7.	Deliver a great performance	Deliver a great experience

Then I thought, how can a band director take a group of 13-year-olds from several area schools and in one week teach them five new music pieces and deliver an outstanding, memorable performance in front of hundreds of people? Here's how we can apply that same success formula.

	Band Director	Medi/Spa Director
1.	Teach them the music	Teach them your experience
2.	Give them direction	Provide training & direction
3.	Listen to how they sound	Listen to the team's communication
4.	Watch band's performance	Watch team behaviors & conduct
5.	Set expectations	Set targets and expectations
6.	Assess performance	Assess & measure performance
7.	Correct or make adjustments	Make adjustments
8.	Hours of additional practice, encouragement	Role play, practice, encouragement

	Band Director	Medi/Spa Director
9.	Hours of additional practice, encouragement	Role play, practice, encouragement
10.	Measure performance	Measure performance – often
11.	Deliver a great performance	Deliver a great experience
12.	Applause & recognition for their work	Recognize them for a job well done

If they can do that in one week with students, why can't we do that with adult professionals? You can! You just need a plan to do it!

Go ahead; rate yourself as the medi/spa director of your team. Are you practicing the above steps to deliver great guest experiences? If you are, congratulations! You must be enjoying a good retention rate, rave reviews, and plenty of referrals. If you are not, what can you do to improve performance?

You see, for Charlie to be chosen as an All County player, he had to practice and perform better than most of his friends and peers who play the tuba, and so did all the other student musicians who were in the All County Band. How much practicing is taking place in your medi/spa? Do you have a training curriculum? Is the schedule posted?

One of my biggest pet peeves is how most team members react when asked to attend training. The first question I hear from medi/spa professionals is they want to know if they are going to get paid for it! That is such a terrible culture… if someone is going to train me and I don't have to pay for it, I would be so excited, asking when and where! We need to make a shift to where teams love training and emphasize the importance of practice and training in order to be excellent at what they do.

The second point I like to make is "role play." Charlie had to go for one week to role play for this performance. They had to sit in their seats and play the music over and over until they got it. He had to do this after school. He didn't whine about it, he just did it.

How much role playing is taking place in your medi/spa? For example, how often do you tell your team to recommend home care so you can increase retail sales or make treatment upgrades so you can increase the volume per guest? Do they do it? In most cases, no. Yet you tolerate it over and over. Suppose you were a band director and you told one of your students to play the music a certain way and they kept playing it their own way. How long do you think they would be in the band? Not long. Are they helping you play your tune and playing it well? Or are they playing their own tune while delivering poor performance?

Now is the time to be excellent at what you do! Be the outstanding director you know you can be and prepare your team to deliver memorable, great performances!

Dori Recommends....

To help you with your business you can tap into the following effective tools:

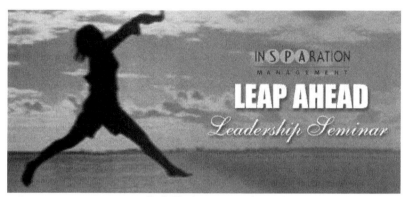

Improve your overall skills by attending the Leap Ahead Medi/Spa Leader Seminar

10 Secrets to Building a High Performance Team

As a medi/spa entrepreneur, one of the most important functions of your position is to recruit, select, and build a high-performance team. You can have the most beautiful medi/spa, but if you don't have the right team working with you, success will only be a dream. Here are 10 secrets to help you build you dream team.

1. Staff vs. TEAM
Many medi/spa leaders call their employees staff. From now on, replace the word staff with TEAM. You don't build a staff, you build a TEAM!

2. Recruiting Efforts
Finding the right fit takes time and effort. You can't wait for potential candidates to come through your door. You need to go on a recruiting mission, just like they do in sports. Recruiters seek out talent and you need to do the same! You should never stop recruiting; always keep your eyes open for talented people. Don't wait until you need team members to start looking. That's too late. You will end up hiring the wrong person just to fill a position.

3. Reviewing Resumes
When you receive a resume, there are a couple of key factors you need to look for:

a. The length of previous employments. If they haven't stayed long in one place, we call those individuals "hoppers." And guess what, they will hop right out of your business, too!

b. Experience and education. If they meet your expectations in education and experience, call them for a phone interview. First, ask them if you can call either their present employer or a previous employer. When you make the reference call, all you need to ask is one question, "Would you rehire this person?"

Most medi/spa owners call references at the end of the interview process. We practice the opposite. Check references *before* you start the interview process. This will save a lot of time and effort. If they pass the reference check, then continue with the interview process. If they don't pass the reference check, on to the next person!

4. Interview Process
Go beyond a gut feeling. Don't hire someone because you like them; that's not enough. We practice "past performance predicts future performance." When you interview someone, you need to ask questions to help you discover how they performed in certain situations.

Here are a couple of sample interview questions: "Tell me about a time when you and your manager disagreed on something. What took place and how was it resolved?" "Tell me about a specific incident where you did not get along with a team member. How did you handle it?"

Be prepared with your interview questions and document your interview process. You need to hire slow and fire fast. If you make it difficult to get a job with your company, you will more likely hire the right person.

5. Position Description
The biggest mistake we encounter is that most medi/spas do not have a detailed position description to give the candidate for a clear outline of what the position entails and what is expected of them. For example, "retail sales" is a big

issue for most medi/spas. Yet, it is rarely discussed in the interview process. Usually after they are hired is when they are told they should recommend retail products. It's too late at that point and that's when all the problems begin. You need to outline *all responsibilities up front*. This step greatly reduces post-hiring problems.

6. Commitment Agreement

This is one of my favorite steps in the hiring process that we detail in the CLARITI Hiring System. Once a position is offered, present a commitment agreement outlining all your key expectations and get them to sign off on it. In the agreement, you should outline what you expect from them and what they can expect from you. This is not a legal document. It's just an internal professional to professional agreement giving clarity to both employee and employer.

7. Training and Development

Now that you have hired your new team member, it's your responsibility to set them up for success and that requires training. What kind of training do you offer new hires? Do you have training manuals? Your training program should focus on developing their technical and business skills.

8. Performance Measures

If you want to have a successful team, you must set targets and measure performance. This is a big problem in our industry. As a consulting firm, we frequently hear from medi/spa owners who are unhappy with their team's performance and want help. When we ask them if they have targets or measure performance, 89% of the time the answer is no. Again, using a sports analogy, can you imagine watching the Super Bowl without keeping score? What would be the point? In sports, they track every move, score, foul, penalty, assist, etc. What should we measure?

Retention, guest satisfaction, volume per guest for service and retail, referral rate, image, work ethic, and team effort.

9. Recognition & Rewards

Many studies have been conducted about the importance of recognition. It's a fact that recognition and appreciation of work well done is the number one factor in team satisfaction. Recognition is motivational. Create a reward program and recognize your team on a monthly basis. This can be as simple as printing a certificate and announcing their achievement during your monthly meeting. You can recognize top achievers: most professional, key player, highest retention rate, and so on.

10. Investing in Education

Last but not least, the most important step of building a high performance team is the commitment to invest in education. This is a key factor for continuous growth. Sad but often true, many medi/spa owners put education on the back burner. Normally, they count on their brands to conduct their training. Though product training is necessary, the key that is often neglected is *business* coaching and training. For example, teaching the team how to:

- Ask for Referrals
- Upgrade Treatments
- Recommend Home Care
- Self-Generate Guests
- Cross-Promote Services & Products
- Increase Retention Rate
- Deliver a Flawless Guest Experience

- Promote Gift Cards
- Treatment Series
- Memberships

If you want a high performance team, you need to invest the time and money in training and coaching. Excellence does not just happen! Look at how much an Olympian goes through to become the best. You need to apply the same effort if you want to be the best. But here is the good news; you don't have to reinvent the wheel. There are business education tools available to help you and your team become the best. Simply reach out, begin implementing, and watch your performance soar!

I would like to share one of the many success stories from professionals who reached out to us for help: Mendel and Jessica Bell, owners of Touch Healing Wellness & Med Spa in North Myrtle Beach, NC. Last month, they broke all their previous performance records. Volume per guest went up from $75 to over a $100! That's a 25% increase in service revenue. Their retail VPG went up by 150%. I am not sharing this to impress you, but to impress upon you that when you invest in yourself and in your team's education, you will elevate your success! Education does pay off!

Dori Recommends....

To help you with your business you can tap into the following effective tools:

Employee Orientation Manual

Four Strategies to Transform your Guest Relations Department

After completing two tele-seminars on how to transform your guest relations department, part of the Spa Management Essentials CoachMe Gold Series, we had so many comments from members regarding the content we shared and how beneficial it was to their team, so I decided to include it in this book.

As far as I am concerned, the guest relations department can make or break your medi/spa. Let's start with the major mistakes medi/spa owners or leaders make in regard to the guest relations department. (Ok, maybe not you....)

Let's start with management mistakes leaders make with the guest relations department.

1. Not having a receptionist – this is a sure way to kill your business. Believe it or not, we still hear that some people don't have a receptionist.

2. Not having formal training for your receptionist or not having a department manual – this is a recipe for lack of consistency, and a disaster waiting to happen.

3. Thinking all you need is someone to answer the phone – order takers instead of revenue generators. Yes, they will answer the phone, but how much money are you losing?

4. Not setting performance targets or expectations for the team – if you don't measure, you can't improve.

5. Getting paid a flat hourly rate – no motivation to excel.

6. Not focusing on sales – we have this phobia about selling, but guess what... if you don't sell, you won't grow.

7. Not having an effective software program.

Avoid Missing Revenue-Generating Opportunities

Last week I conducted a secret shopper medi/spa assessment and I have to tell you, the medi/spa receptionist totally missed the boat. It started with my assistant making the reservation.

- They did not attempt to recommend multiple treatments to me.
- When I checked in, they failed to recommend another treatment again.
- When I checked out, they failed to ask for my next medi/spa appointment. They did not discuss boutique items with me. They did not ask me to complete a guest comment card, nor did they ask for my testimonial.

Oh my... I was impressed. Not!

Invest in Training the Guest Relations Team

Training the team is essential to the success of any medi/spa business.

- Have structure, systems, and strategies in place
- Develop all your scripts
- Have role-play meetings
- Test their knowledge on products and treatments
- Outline your sales approach and training

Maximize Medi/Spa Revenue

It is the responsibility of the guest relations team to maximize revenue through call management, check-in, and check-out. When the team has a target to reach for number of treatments, service volume, retail volume, gift cards sold, etc., they are more likely to reach their goal and hit their target.

Reward and Recognize Efforts

Recognizing the team will go a long way. Conduct monthly meetings to recognize your team and encourage them to stay on the right path.

These are all the essential steps to ensure your medi/spa guest relations department is performing up to par.

During the Spa Management Essentials tele-seminars, I spoke directly to receptionists and gave them strategies they can implement immediately. We discussed how to tap into revenue opportunities that will help the medi/spa be more efficient and more successful.

I was speaking with Cheri Satterfield, an InSPAration Management client who owns Tuscan Sun (two locations) in West Virginia, and she told me that changing one thing has made a huge difference in the receptionist process. That one thing was reserving time instead of specific treatments, especially for facials. She said that helps the receptionists simplify the reservation process and allows the therapists to select the ideal treatment for the guests. The guests win, the team wins, and the medi/spa wins. Everyone is happy.

Cheri is a Leap Ahead graduate. I visited her and did her Fresh Start, where we trained her team and changed the compensation model. She is also a CoachMe Gold Member and a Done for Me Marketing member. Her business has grown 50%+ over the last year.

There is a saying that says, "What got you here won't get you to the next level." You see, people like Cheri know that, and that's why she participates in all the business tools we offer.

You can grow, too! We encourage you to join the Spa Management Essentials series.

Building Trust

It is not surprising that study after study shows a decline in the trust that we have in business and political leaders, and in personal life. The Edelman Trust Study found that nearly two out of every three adults surveyed in 20 countries trust corporations and businesses less now.

Even though we are faced with a crisis in trust and have ample examples of how lack of trust ruins relationships, I am a firm believer that we can work on trust and build lasting relationships with everyone around us by being trustworthy in someone's eyes. Trust is based on perceptions and needs to be earned through good and honest communication and behavior.

About a year ago we noticed a cat coming around our house. She obviously did not have a home. We began to feed her, but every time we got near her she would hiss at us and she backed up to protect herself and avoid harm. This went on for a couple of weeks. Then she began to trust. She loved being around our house and now she comes up to us. Not once has she hissed at us again. Of course, Charlie named her. Meet Felix. You see, you have to earn trust from everyone, even animals.

Trust is very powerful and it's one of the main pillars of any healthy relationship. When trust exists between husband and wife, family members, clients and your business, you and your team, you and your pet, and so on, it results in lasting relationships. But if trust is broken, the relationship is usually tarnished and you have to work very hard to repair it, assuming it can be repaired.

In business, we all work very hard to obtain a new client and then we do everything we can to retain them. Or we hire a new team member and pray that they will be good and they will stay. Sometimes we succeed and sometimes we don't. Let's face it, we all need to build lasting relationships to be more successful. Here are some tips on how you can apply TRUST in your daily life.

T. Transparent

Be transparent. People will trust you more when they see and understand why you are making certain decisions. The more transparent you are with information, the more your medi/spa team will understand why you do what you do. Communicate as openly as you can about decisions, processes, and changes.

Encourage your team to participate openly in as many decisions as possible. By allowing them to ask questions and offer you their ideas, you demonstrate that you care about their input. If your team feels you're not really hearing what they have to say, you'll find it hard to gain their trust.

R. Reputation

"Build a strong reputation. You can't build a reputation on what you are going to do."
- Henry Ford

Building a good reputation and earning your team's and your clients' respect plays a large role in gaining trust.

Focus on building a great self-image and reputation. Reputation is about what others believe to be true about your character, personality, skills, competencies, and values. People develop an opinion of these things based on behavior. When you leave a positive impression, you open up many doors of opportunity. Don't let a bad reputation break trust and close doors or even alienate others.

U. Understanding

"Seek First to Understand and Then to Be Understood," is the 5th habit in the book *7 Habits of Highly Effective People* by Stephen Covey.

Communication is the most important skill in life. You spend years learning how to read and write, and years learning how to speak. What about listening?

If you're like most people, you probably seek first to be understood; you want to get your point across. And in doing so, you may ignore the other person completely, pretend that you're listening, selectively hear only certain parts of the conversation, or attentively focus on only the words being said, but miss the meaning entirely. This behavior does not promote trust. If you focus on listening and understanding the other person's point of view first, this behavior will help you build trust and long lasting relationships.

S. Satisfaction

Exceed client expectations. Trust is related to client and team satisfaction. We all have internal and external customers. As a leader it's your responsibility to ensure the satisfaction of both. When that occurs, you establish trust. Make customer satisfaction a strategic priority for your business.

Communicate clear guest service expectations and paint a picture of how great your guest will look and feel. Recognize and reward your team for their delivery of a great guest experience. Resolve client complaints quickly. Measure guest and team satisfaction as a gauge of how well internal and external customer needs are being met.

T. Training

Continually participate in training. It takes training to ensure that trust is strong between your organization and your clients.

Earn the trust of your clients by insisting that everyone observe the "Five Pillars of Trust." They Include:

1. Deliver on your promises.
2. Go out of your way to help.
3. Anticipate and fulfill needs.
4. Make it easy for guests to do business with you.
5. Be consistent.

Trust is power. It's the power to inspire and influence. It's the glue that bonds us to each other, that strengthens relationships, and that creates a strong chain. Build trust and you'll build a strong medi/spa business!

Medi/Spa Team Motivation

While recently conducting a preliminary coaching session with a new client who owns a very large medi/spa, I sensed an unhappy tone in her voice as she began to express to me how bad her team's morale is. She said, "They are lazy, no one likes their job, they do the minimum, they don't like me or my management style, and the list goes on and on. Please help me!"

That conversation got me thinking... how does the team get to this point? How do things get so bad? This does not happen overnight. When people take a new job, they are usually excited and happy for the opportunity they are given. That period is known as the honeymoon period. Then, things begin to change. Slowly, the person gets disengaged and usually quits weeks before they tell you they are leaving. What can you do to keep the honeymoon attitude going and avoid a divorce?

Usually, *employees don't quit jobs, they quit managers*. If you are experiencing a revolving door, it's time to look at your management style and see what you need to change or improve to keep your team motivated and engaged.

To improve relations and communication between medi/spa leaders and the team, it's important to know the different behavioral styles that exist within your medi/spa. There are four behavioral styles:

1. *The director* – Pushy, a "get to the point" kind of person.
2. *The thinker* – Very detail oriented, they dot all the "I"s and cross all the "T"s.
3. *The socializer* – Likes to talk and have fun.

4. *The mediator* – Does not like change; a very touchy, feely kind of person.

Here is the problem:

1. Many therapists are right-brained people and fit in the mediator behavioral style. They are very sensitive. They are people-oriented, mellow, like things calm, and they resist change.

2. Many medi/spa directors or medi/spa owners have a director behavioral style. They are straight shooters and don't beat around the bush. They are perceived as pushy, money-driven, uncaring, and so on.

When you get these two styles together, the relationship will start out good, but quickly changes. Why? Because the director's true colors come through, making the mediator style very unhappy.

To make this relationship work, the leader has to learn to flex their style while communicating with the mediator style in order to maintain a positive work environment and retain employees.

Remember, you are the leader. Control your behavior and influence your team. If you need help, get a coach or a mentor. Read books on leadership (John Maxwell has many helpful books on this subject). Or contact a consulting firm to assist you.

How Much Team Business Training Should You Do?

It depends... are you going for the gold or settling for coal?

While conducting the Seven Steps to Economical Marketing webinar for Pevonia partners, I took some questions from the participants. One question in particular got my attention. The question was, "Dori, you mentioned training the team and that marketing is a team effort. How much training should someone provide the team or how much time should a manager spend on training?"

Unfortunately, we were almost out of time, but I was able to give her the short version. My answer was, "It all depends on the current skill level your team has. If they are doing a great job and delivering the results you are expecting, then you only need 'brush-up training' once every two weeks or so. If your team and your medi/spa are not operating at the capacity you think they should be operating at, roll up your sleeves and start training! You need to train as much as you can until your goals are achieved."

In working with many medi/spas, the lack of a business training plan is one of the biggest issues we frequently encounter.

Here are seven steps to improve your training efforts:
1. Assign a specific person to be in charge of training
2. Assess your training needs
3. Develop a training curriculum
4. Publish a training schedule

5. Evaluate your training and measure effectiveness
6. Be consistent
7. Develop departmental training in writing (manual)

For most medi/spas, training is usually conducted by the brand they carry. Very rarely do we see internal business training conducted within the medi/spa.

As many of you may know, business training is my passion... If you are looking to improve your organization's bottom line and performance, there is only one way to achieve results and that is through training. I often use sports analogies when it comes to training subjects. Take a look at an Olympian. For example, Michael Phelps, who won 14 gold medals. How much did he train? 40 hours per week. If you want to reach excellence, you have to invest money and time in training. That is the only way to get the gold!

Back to the question, "how often should you train?" As often as possible... until you reach excellence! Or until your team knows how to:

- Upgrade and maximize the volume per guest
- Ask for and obtain referrals
- Recommend retail products consistently
- Self-market their services
- Cross-market your products and services
- Increase retention rate
- Deliver a *Wow!* guest experience
- Be confident about product knowledge
- Operate at full capacity

I encourage you to set training goals for your organization and your team. Begin investing time and money in effective business training programs. Today, more than ever, education has become very economical via webinars.

Dori Recommends….

InSPAration Management offers advanced business webinars for only $750 for the entire team! Sign up and invite your entire team to attend. Combine internal and external professional training, and collect your GOLD!

Need help with training? Contact:
info@ InSPArationManagement.com

How to Address Mental Health in the Medi/Spa Workplace

The phrase "Mental Health" in the work environment is usually a result of job stress and/or burnout, communication or the need for conflict resolution between employees, or employee anxiety.

We think because we are in the medi/spa industry we don't get stressed. The fact is many employers and employees in the medi/spa industry rarely go to medi/spas or practice what they preach. Is this a cry for help? Daily, we receive indicators that many are stressed. What efforts are you making to resolve these issues?

Mental health is one of the hottest business topics today. This makes it a great opportunity for all medi/spa owners to improve employees' state of health and increase revenue by developing programs to help other industries and generate new revenue streams.

Did you know…

- More than 90% of employees agree that their mental health and personal problems spill over into their professional lives and have a direct impact on their job performance.

- Stress in the workplace causes approximately one million employees to miss work every day!

- Three out of four employees who seek treatment for workplace issues or mental health problems experience an increase in work performance.

Are your employees actively engaged in their work? Recently a Gallup study found that only 26% of employees surveyed categorized themselves as actively engaged in their work. Studies illustrate that there is a direct relationship between employee engagement, leadership, and retention.

A mental health friendly workplace makes good business sense. It benefits everyone... employees, employers, and the bottom line. Healthy minds have many benefits:

• **Higher Productivity and Motivation.** If you care about your team's well-being, they will feel valued and secure, and be more productive.

• **Reduced Absenteeism.** Workplace stress is a major cause of absenteeism. Helping employees manage their stress and overall mental health will boost productivity.

• **Loyalty and Retention.** Reduce turnover cost along with cost savings in recruitment, new employee orientation, and training.

• **Hiring the Right Team.** Practice behavioral interview questions, not your typical, traditional process.

• **Position Clarity.** This helps reduce stress and anxiety by making responsibilities clear.

• **Better Workplace Relations.** Open communication channels to express situations. Create a positive climate for understanding, conflict resolution, and support.

Develop a corporate wellness program and then offer it to companies in your community. You can help them offer their employees methods to maintain a healthier state of mind while opening new streams of revenue and opportunity for everyone.

Five Steps to an Effective Medi/Spa Tour

When was the last time you took a medi/spa tour where you were impressed with the presentation and the person who toured you? I don't know about you, but it's been a while for me. As a matter of fact, many medi/spas don't even want to give tours anymore. I walked into a large resort spa in Vegas not too long ago and asked for a tour. They looked at me as if I had two heads! They told me, *"Sorry, we don't tour because clothing is optional."* I replied, *"You don't give your guests robes? Are they running around naked?"* Just tell me no instead of giving some fictional reason.

I don't know about you, but if I am going to pay $185 for a massage, I want to see the place first. I hope that you are not one of those medi/spas that refuses to give tours. Giving a tour is a marketing strategy. When people see your place and you present it properly, they will make reservations.

Many medi/spas give tours and focus on telling instead of selling. For example, they walk around saying, *"This is our facial room, this is our massage room,* etc..." That's telling. What you need to present is, *"In this facial suite, you can experience all types of effective facials from anti-aging to corrective to Microdermabrasion."* Focus on the treatment and the experience instead of the room! We are not selling real estate, we are selling medi/spa experiences! In this section, you will discover five easy steps on conducting effective medi/spa tours that result in a reservation.

1. Greeting Guests
A welcome with a big smile always makes a great first impression and sets the tone for the tour. Instead of saying, "May I help you?" consider, "Are you here for your experience or to reserve one?"

2. Introduction - Mini Commercial

Introduce yourself and the medi/spa. Do you have a mini commercial? Here is an example for you: While in the boutique area or reception you can say, *"The Medi/Spa is a full service medi/spa, rated as one of the top medi/spas in the area. We feature holistic and all natural treatments and products. A vast selection of experiences are designed to address skin care concerns for face, body, hands, and feet. Guests who frequent the medi/spa experience the ultimate de-stressing rituals combined with result-driven treatments."*

3. Menu

"Here is the menu. In it, you will find a variety of treatments. Allow me to show you the medi/spa."

4. The Tour

You should conduct the tour the same way they would experience the medi/spa. Tell a story. It is best to script the tour. This way everyone will deliver the same tour, providing consistency.

Begin with the changing lounge. I'm not going to script the whole thing for you, but here is a little sample: *"The first thing we will do when you are here for your experience is bring you to the Changing Lounge so you can slip into these very comfortable slippers and a cozy robe."* (Show locker) *Next, you should enjoy the amenities. Here we have a sauna, steam, and specialty showers. They are all here for you to use and enjoy prior to your treatments!*

"Then, you will go into the Relaxation Lounge where you can enjoy medi/spa refreshments. This will help you relax and prepare you for your treatment.
"One of the medi/spa's professional team members will escort you to the Treatment Suite, where outstanding guest experiences are designed to exceed your expectations!"

5. Asking for the Reservation

Now that you have toured the medi/spa and presented your medi/spa experiences, it is time to ask, *"What type of treatments would you like to experience?"* Suggest something like, *"Let me share with you the most popular package."* It should include at least two treatments. Always think packages! Two treatments or more to start, then go a la carte. You need to ask for the reservation. This is the biggest mistake many medi/spa teams make. They show the entire medi/spa but fail to ask, *"Which package would you like to experience?"* or, *"When would you like to come and experience these treatments?"* We have to ask, and when we ask, we receive! But the frequent problem is, we simply don't ask!

Follow this structure and you will give great tours, enticing your guests to make the reservation and increase your revenue!

Dori Recommends....

To help you with your business you can tap into the following effective tools:

Guest Relations Manual & Audio

Recipes For Success

Chapter 5:

Hiring and Training a High Performance Medi/Spa Team

"Start with good people, lay out the rules, communicate with your employees, motivate them, and reward them. If you do all those things effectively, you can't miss."
- Lee Iacocca

Five Steps to Help You Build Your Medi/Spa Dream Team

One of the biggest challenges medi/spa leaders are faced with is team issues. We hear so many complaints about lack of motivation, dedication, bad attitudes, not going the extra mile, wanting everything delivered on a silver platter, and so on... Does this sound familiar? Yes, but how can we change it? How can we build a dream team?

Building a high performance team starts with the hiring process. The problem we often encounter is that most people hire fast and fire slow. It should be the opposite. You need to *hire slow and fire fast*. Here are five steps to help build your dream team.

1. Recruiting Mission
Finding the right fit takes time. You can't wait for people to come to you. You need to go on a recruiting mission, just like they do in sports. You need to keep your eyes open for talented people. Don't wait until you need people to start looking. You need to be looking all the time and have people in your pipeline. Looking for people when you need them is too late! You end up hiring the wrong person just to fill a position.

2. Interview Process
Go beyond a gut feeling. Don't hire someone because you like them; that's not enough. You need to go through a complete interview process. You want to make it difficult to get a job with your company.

3. Position Description
The biggest mistake we see is that most medi/spas do not have a detailed position description to give the candidate

for a clear outline of what the position is all about and what is expected. For example, retail sales are a big issue for most of you. Yet, it's rarely discussed in the interview process. You wait until you hire them and then you say, "I want you to do this and that." It is too late at that point, and that's when all the problems begin. You need to outline *all responsibilities upfront*. This step greatly reduces post-hiring problems.

4. Commitment Agreement

This is one of my favorite steps of the hiring process. Once you make the position offer, you need to present a commitment agreement outlining all the points that drive you crazy *now* and get them to sign off on it. In the agreement, you should put what you expect from them and what they can expect from you. This is not a legal document. It's just an internal professional to professional agreement giving clarity to both of you.

5. Training and Development

Now that you have hired your new team member, it's your responsibility to set them up for success, and that requires training. What kind of training do you offer your new hires? Do you have training manuals to help you? Your training program should focus on developing their technical *and* business skills.

Implement these five steps to build your medi/spa dream team!

Are You Setting Up Your Medi/Spa Team for Success or Failure?

In the past I have used a taxi driver analogy to illustrate the fact that they leave their home not knowing where they are going to end up and how some people are running their business in the same manner. They show up to work, wonder what they are going to be doing today, and react to what comes their way. Are you a taxi driver or are you a leader?

Leaders know where they want to go! They have a clear vision, a plan for their business and their team. Which brings me to the question the title of this article poses: are you setting up your medi/spa team for success or failure? In most cases, people get hired and they learn about the products and maybe the protocols or rituals, if the medi/spa happens to have some....

What's wrong with this picture? Lack of business training, lack of revenue-generating focus, and lack of strategic planning on how to reach clearly defined goals!

Here are few essential tips to building a high-performance team.

1. Medi/Spa Structure
The first thing you need to know is that you cannot do everything yourself. You need help! At a minimum, you will need help from a manager, supervisor, or team leader and a well-defined organizational structure. It's essential to have a growth plan that defines the efforts of your management team. As a leader, commit to business education and invest the time and money in someone who will help you grow and build your business. If you don't have an organizational

structure, it's time to create one and share it with your team.

Once you have identified the person for your management team, they can help you train, coach, manage, plan, organize, grow, and more... but *only* if you set them up for success! They need training *before* they start training others. Only then will you ensure your success!

2. Department Manuals

Some people work way too hard constantly trying to reinvent the wheel rather than documenting what works and having a manual to train and retrain their team. It's like being an actor. You are handed a script for a role in a play. If you want to be in the play, you have to learn the role. If you don't learn the script, they will get someone else. However, here is the thing, when they hire another actor, they don't change the script. The script is still the same, only the person changes. Unfortunately, in many medi/spas I see people changing and the scripts are changing, too... big mistake! It's time to create your scripts. You need a department manual so you can have a successful play!

3. Team Performance Standards

While in NY at the spa show, I was speaking with a husband and wife team who own a very nice spa in New Hampshire. I met them last year and they bought several of the Success Library USBs. They implemented many strategies and are doing very well! Although Jim was telling me how he is unsatisfied with one of his receptionists. She is great at guest service but can't sell anything.

So I asked him, "Does she have goals?" He said, "Yes!" "Is she getting a bonus for selling over and above her hourly rate?" He said, "Yes!" "Are there consequences for not reaching goals?" He said, "No."

So, there you go... You must have team performance standards and consequences if they don't reach performance expectations. Let's go back to our actor example: If the actor is lousy and can't memorize his/her lines, how long do you think he/she will remain on the show? You can't afford to keep anyone who is not meeting performance expectations, as they are costing *you* business! Every team member in every department must have performance standards and understand the consequences for poor performance.

Dori Recommends....

To help you with your business you can tap into the following effective tools:

Genius Marketing and Sales Strategies

Medi/Spa Prima Donna... Who, Me?

While visiting a client at her spa recently, I couldn't help but notice a particular person on her spa team that fit the prototypical "Prima Donna" characteristics. It got me thinking about that label, "Prima Donna." The term is commonly used to describe someone who behaves in a demanding, often temperamental fashion, revealing an inflated view of themselves, their talent, and their importance. They are usually vain, undisciplined, egotistical, and very difficult to work with.

Am I describing someone on your medi/spa team? Probably, because most teams have one. Don't take this the wrong way, but are *you* that person in your company?

Most of us want respect at work, but we have to earn it! All of us, at one time or another, have been dissatisfied when things didn't go our way. Remember, we don't live in a perfect world. We gain respect through our behaviors and actions. Here are five tips to help reform the "Prima Donna" attitude.

1. **"That's not my job."** Stop and understand why you've been asked to do certain tasks. Maybe your leader wants you to do it because you are good at it. Take it as a compliment. Saying yes will get you up the ladder a lot faster than saying no or fussing about it. Are you looking at your position as a job or a career? Saying yes is the way to climb the ladder!

2. **"It's not my fault."** If there's a problem, fix it. It does not matter whose fault it is. If you did, in fact, screw up... own up to it. Then come up with a solution as quickly as you can. It's ok to make mistakes. It's not ok to point fingers at someone else, especially if you are at fault.

3. "It's not my problem." If a crisis is brewing, pitch in and help. If you don't have anything constructive to say, silence is golden at a time like this.

4. "It won't work." Being closed-minded is one of the worst qualities a person can have. Shutting an idea down before it even gets developed is counterproductive. Open up your mind and give new strategies an opportunity, even if they seem impossible. We need to search for ways to make it happen... and then boldly chart a new path.

5. "I am way over-qualified for this job." Maybe you are. But, the fact is, this is the job you have. You agreed to take it on. Complaining that you're too good for it only makes you look bad. And guess what? You're not going to make your leader think, "This is a superior person. I need to promote him/her."

If you are a Prima Donna, it's time to change your ways. Go ahead, become a superstar! Exceed the expectation and you will receive the respect you deserve.

Shifting the Medi/Spa Retail Philosophy from Selling to Recommending!

Therapists: "You want me to do what?" The number one battle facing your business is the lack of retail sales and upgrade opportunities. As a manager or owner, you know how significant retail sales and upgrades are to your profit line. Unfortunately, your team may not share that same understanding. What can you do to improve revenue generation, especially during these difficult economic times? Hold a team meeting and explain the following facts to your team.

Fact 1: The Difference Between Selling and Recommending.

Selling is convincing someone to buy something whether they need it or not.

Recommending is providing a solution to a specific problem or concern.

Fact 2: Studies Indicate Consumers go to Medi/Spas to:

1. Relax and de-stress
2. Look and feel better - looking for results
3. Become educated on how to live the medi/spa lifestyle
4. *Learn about new treatments/products*

Fact 3: An Average Person Uses 12 Different Products per Day.

Guests use products, too. So if everybody buys products, which products should they purchase? Department store products, drug store products, or professional products found in medi/spas? (Does your team believe their medi/spa products are better than department store products? Do they use their own medi/spa's products?)

Fact 4: Guests are Seeking:
- Result-driven treatments
- Knowledgeable and skilled therapists
- Living the medi/spa lifestyle by taking the medi/spa experience home
- To receive *professional* advice

Fact 5: Guests Who Purchase Products from the Medi/Spa Visit the Spa More Often.

The product provides a link back to the therapist and the medi/spa.

Fact 6: Our Professional Obligation is to Fulfill Our Guests' Needs and Offer a Complete Experience.

Is your team doing that? What is a complete medi/spa experience? A complete guest experience contains two steps:

1. Perform a result-driven treatment in the medi/spa
2. Educate your guests and offer recommendations on how to maintain a medi/spa lifestyle at home

Shift the philosophy within your medi/spa. It's not about selling products; it's about recommending solutions to concerns your guests have. Many therapists tell us they chose a career in the medi/spa industry to help people. Are they really helping your guests by letting them go and figure out on their own what products they should use between treatments?

Fact 7: Remind Your Team They are Licensed Professionals.

They earned the right and own the responsibility to make professional recommendations to their guests. It's their professional obligation!

What can you do as a manager?

Discuss all the facts above with your team and help shift the philosophy of how they view retail within your medi/spa. It's about recommending, *not* selling! To boost retail sales, you will need to provide your team with a recommending system.

If you work on shifting the philosophy of how your team views retail, you will improve your guest experience and increase revenue.

Dori Recommends….

To help you with your business you can tap into the following effective tools:

Increase Revenue With P.R.I.D.E. Manual

Medi/Spa Reception - Reservation & Profits

Do you recall the last time you called a medi/spa to reserve a medi/spa experience and the person who answered the phone was so knowledgeable and professional that you said, "Wow! That was a great first impression of the medi/spa!" Or, if you operate a medi/spa, when did one of your clients give you a compliment on how well your receptionist and/or reservationist conducted themselves? If it's been a while, maybe it's time to take a closer look.

After a long and busy business trip, I decided to extend my stay and visit the medi/spa for some treatments. My hotel room did not have a medi/spa menu (mistake # 1), so I had to call the medi/spa to discover treatment options.

The person answering the phone greeted me with "Hello, thanks for calling XYZ medi/spa, can you please hold?" There was not a hold message informing callers of menu options (mistake #2). After holding for a while, she came back and said, "Thank you for holding. How may I help you?"

I asked the person (she did not give her name, mistake #3) to tell me about some of their treatment options. As many receptionists do, the first thing she mentioned is massage, facials, and body treatments. Then I asked, "What body treatment would you suggest to relieve stress and dry skin?" "Probably our mud body wrap," she said.

"Can you tell me a little more about it?" That's when every other word was "um" and "like" and "you know." Her lack of communication skill and treatment knowledge was obvious (mistake # 4). I could tell that this person was not properly trained, nor had she experienced any of the medi/spa treatments herself (mistake #5). Her description and verbiage were not medi/spa-driven. She had no structure for handling the call or the ability to describe the treatment benefits to entice the caller to reserve an experience. Her recommendations in selecting treatments and promoting the medi/spa menu were very limited (mistake #6).

Who is held accountable for the delivery of this type of experience: the employee or the medi/spa's leadership?

Is your R & R department making or breaking you?

Sad but true, this is not the first time I've experienced this type of call. I am sure you have experienced the same. Maybe it's time to re-assess your guest relations and reservation department. What do your receptionist and/or reservationist contribute to deliver a great guest experience and maximize your reservation rate?

Fact: In most medi/spas, the guest relations and reservation department is usually regarded as entry level or lower positions within the medi/spa structure (mistake # 7), even though both of these departments are key revenue-generating centers. Shift philosophy and place greater emphasis on selecting and training the team. Recruiting and maintaining skilled professionals will result in maximized revenues and increased profits!

If your R & R department needs to improve their productivity and increase the reservation and revenue rate, it's time to implement these four steps to building a successful R & R team.

1. **R & R Role Identification – Finding the Right Fit**
   First, identify the ideal characteristics and skills required for your R & R positions. Then, create a detailed position description for both the receptionist and the reservationist.

Note: R & R position qualification must go beyond the ability to pick up the phone and say hello. They must be able to maximize revenue by promoting the medi/spa's services and products. Stay away from order takers; instead, seek achievers. Many medi/spas still do not have position descriptions (mistake #8).

2. **R & R Compensation Structure**

While conversing with a medi/spa owner recently, the owner expressed her disappointment with her medi/spa receptionists' and reservationists' performances. She went on to tell me, "I don't understand why they don't attempt to upgrade services, promote packages, schedule future appointments, or increase retail sales... especially when I just gave them all a raise!" I asked her if the raise was based on performance targets and she said no. My reply to her was, "What motivation does your team have to improve their performance if their pay is the same no matter what their performance is? What compensation plan do you offer your R & R team?"

In most medi/spas, the R & R department is paid a straight salary (mistake # 9). This is one of the biggest faux pas you can make since R & R controls revenue generation. Instead, consider a compensation structure based on targets and performance.

Natalie Spencer, general manager for Spa Renaissance in Fayetteville, North Carolina, oversees two spas. Her R & R structure includes receptionists at the spa and reservationists at an off-site call center. Since she adapted a new compensation structure based on performance and targets, her R & R department experienced a 30% reservation rate increase.

Compensation structure should be based on your overall monthly budget. Assign each person a target and base a higher compensation rate when they reach it and lower the rate if they don't meet or exceed the target. The compensation structure should include a mix of salary, commission, bonus, and benefits.

Compensation Mix

A compensation structure that promotes stretching, goal-setting, and performance awareness results in elevated income opportunities for the team and the medi/spa.

It's a win-win. The team will have the opportunity to increase their income and the medi/spa will only pay the higher level of compensation when the team achieves their targets. Change your medi/spa's R & R compensation plan from straight salary to a compensation mix and witness a performance transformation while generating a new level of success.

3. **R & R Structure and Positioning**
    Depending on the size of your medi/spa, you may want to differentiate between the two positions. The receptionist's

responsibilities should include guest relations and tending to the front desk. The reservationists' responsibility should focus on phone calls and communication management. It is ideal to separate the two by moving the reservation department to an offsite call center or to a different location within the medi/spa. This allows the receptionist to focus on guest relations and the delivery of a great medi/spa experience. The off-site call center can focus on converting callers into guests and maximize the medi/spa's revenue.

If separating the two is not an option due to your medi/spa size, then consider having two or more people (depending on your guest flow) at the front desk: one to focus on calls and one to attend to the guest reception.

All medi/spas strive to deliver a great and unique medi/spa experience. When your receptionist and reservationist positions overlap, it makes it difficult to perform their functions and takes away from the overall guest experience. Not differentiating between R & R positions creates confusion and low productivity (mistake #10).

4. **R & R Department Training**

   Training and coaching the R & R department is an essential component to retaining a professional and successful team. When your reservation and guest relations department is trained and skilled, they are able to maximize reservation rate while increasing overall revenue generation.

   Not having a training manual (mistake #11) is like building a house without a blueprint: you can do it, but it will tumble in time. Having a training manual can make everyone's job a lot easier. It can be the difference between working smarter instead of harder. By investing the time in creating a manual, you are investing in the future of your business. The R & R manual should include scripts, operating guidelines, systems, structures, reservation management steps, software hints and shortcuts, marketing your services and products, treatment benefits, dos and don'ts, and more.

By implementing these four steps, you will transform your R & R department from order takers to movers and shakers! Find the right fit, train them, implement a performance-driven compensation plan, and maximize your revenue while enhancing your guests' experience. Don't delay; seek professional advice to assist with your medi/spa's transition. You can choose from many options:

- Hire a consultant or a coach to assist with training and transition
- Purchase a proven, effective compensation plan
- Attend a reservation and guest relations seminar

Keep in mind that the guest experience begins with the first, "hello." Ask a friend to call your medi/spa, listen to your R & R department, and discover where you stand. Take the following assessment and improve performance.

Score calculation:
4: Strongly Agree
3: Agree
2: Somewhat Agree
1: Disagree

1. The R & R department has a very clear knowledge of the medi/spa's services and products.
   Strongly Agree   Agree   Somewhat Agree   Disagree

2. The R & R team has experienced some of the medi/spa's services and uses medi/spa products.
   Strongly Agree   Agree   Somewhat Agree   Disagree

3. The R & R department is clear on their performance expectations and targets.
Strongly Agree   Agree   Somewhat Agree   Disagree

4. The R & R department has a training manual and scripts to assist them with their position.
Strongly Agree   Agree   Somewhat Agree   Disagree

5. The R & R department is able to professionally communicate with guests and the medi/spa team.
Strongly Agree   Agree   Somewhat Agree   Disagree

6. The R & R team has guest relations experience and sales experience.
Strongly Agree   Agree   Somewhat Agree   Disagree

7. The R & R team is skilled and proficient with the medi/spa's software program.
Strongly Agree   Agree   Somewhat Agree   Disagree

8. The R & R team portrays a professional medi/spa image.
Strongly Agree   Agree   Somewhat Agree   Disagree

9. The R & R team tracks call source and marketing efforts.
Strongly Agree   Agree   Somewhat Agree   Disagree

10. The R & R team realizes the importance of their contribution to the overall success of the medi/spa.
Strongly Agree   Agree   Somewhat Agree   Disagree

Score scale:
31 - 40: Congratulations! Your team is highly skilled!
21 - 30: Your team is average. With some additional training, they could move from good to great!
11 – 20: Your team needs improvement and professional coaching.

10: Evaluate your current team and make necessary changes.

Dori Recommends….

To help you with your business you can tap into the following effective tools:

Guest Relations USB

Never Stop Being a Student!

Many students recently graduated. They have spent years being students. Some are good students and maybe some are not so good. Again, the good old 80/20 rule applies. The top 20% are probably great students and the rest are average. Being a great student carries on throughout a person's career.

Some people never open another book, attend a seminar, or listen to an educational USB once they graduate. Others continue their educational journey. Which one are you?

Well, if you are reading this, you are in the top 20%. Obviously, you want to be a good student. As a coach, I run across good students and not-so-good students. The good ones improve on their business all the time. The not-so-good students have good intentions, but they get distracted easily.

Assess how good of a student you are.
1. Are you even a student?
2. Are you a good student?
3. Are you a great student?
4. Are you an average student?

How can you improve and become a great student? Improving is possible when you have a coach! A business coach helps you identify your goals, stay focused, offers advice, holds you accountable, and ensures that you succeed.

Learn more about an economical yet very effective way to have a coach by becoming a CoachMe (InSPArationManagement.com/coachme-memberships) member.

Education = Success

When I was a little girl, my mom always stressed to all of us how important a good education would be and how it could affect our lives. You probably say the same to your kids, but here is the thing... are you practicing what you are preaching to your kids?

Let's have a moment of truth. How much time do you designate to your business education? We have many professionals in the InSPAration Management community who are great students. They set aside time to learn and dive into Biztools such as the Medi/Spa Success Library (found at www.InSPArationManagement.com/Biztools); CoachMe Platinum, Gold, and Silver; webinars; etc. But not enough people do that. Do you know the phrase, "There is always room at the top?" Well, I want to invite you to be part of the top.

You see, to get to the top you have to be committed to education and be hungry for knowledge. Being a student not only helps you learn new strategies to improve your business, but it also helps you become a better teacher for your team.

I was watching Oprah's "Mastery" episode one night where she was telling her story about how she started out and how she became who she is today. In one part of the show, she was talking about how each episode she did taught her something and made her a better person. *She loved learning and by learning she became a teacher.* She said the reason she never had children is because she chose to be a teacher instead. If you dedicate yourself to being a great student, you will automatically become a great teacher. As a medi/spa leader, you need to be both a student and a teacher! Are you both? Through education, anything is possible.

Here are some tips on how to become a student again:
- Find a buddy to learn with
- Schedule weekly time to sit and learn
- Tap into audio programs such as The CoachMe Memberships
- Build a Success Library – Books, CDs, USBs
- Turn your car into a university by listening to educational CDs or USBs

Once you are a student, you can work on being a teacher for your team. The more everyone learns, the more everyone will earn!

Dori Recommends....

To help you with your business you can tap into the following effective tools:

Join the CoachMe Programs and maintain a competitive advantage. To learn more about the CoachMe Programs, visit:

www.InSPArationManagement.com

Who is Your Medi/Spa Coach?

Coaching is no longer limited to sports. Over 80% of Fortune 500 companies provide professional coaching to their management team. Through coaching, companies and individuals increase profits, grow market shares, and achieve greater success! If you wish to succeed in business and build a high performance team, you must be a coach.

The next time you are watching a basketball or a football game, notice how similar the responsibilities are of a sports head coach and a medi/spa director. Medi/spa professionals can learn many useful strategies from the sports coaching model.

Behind every great team is a great coach!

Who is the head coach for your organization? Who is coaching your team to excellence?

Professional sports teams spend millions of dollars developing their coaching business models. They are time-tested and have proven to be effective. Let's explore the sports coaching model and discover which components can be applied to your medi/spa coaching model.

1. **TEAM - *Sports Coaching Model***
   The first thing you should notice about a sports organization is that they call their personnel a "TEAM." An acronym for TEAM is "Together Everyone Achieves More."

   TEAM - *Medi/Spa Coaching Model*
   In the medi/spa industry, most medi/spa operators call their personnel "STAFF." It is time to replace the word staff with TEAM! Become a TEAM with a name and an identity. Instill

unity, promote teamwork and purpose within your team, and together everyone will achieve more!

2. **Structure - *Sports Coaching Model***
Now that you have a team, it is time for team structure. The sports model has players, team leaders, assistant coaches, support personnel, a marketing and sales team, operations team, and of course, a head coach. Each person has a clear position description and definition, responsibilities and accountabilities, with a goal and a mission to win games.

Structure - *Medi/Spa Coaching Model*
The medi/spa head coach must detail the medi/spa team structure and define each team member's role and responsibilities, purpose, and goals. The objective of the medi/spa is to deliver a memorable medi/spa experience and increase volume per guest while improving the guest retention rate. Within the medi/spa team structure, the coaching team is responsible for providing clarity and guidelines to accomplish goals and maximize performance.

3. **Recruiting - *Sports Coaching Model***
"Team building is all about recruiting and getting the right people on the bus" (Jim Collins, *Good to Great*). Each sports team has starters and backups. Starters are the stars. They account for most of the team's production per game. This is where the 80/20 rule generally applies; 80% of your business is normally generated by 20% of your team. Professional teams focus highly on recruiting and scouting, continuously searching for new stars. The head coach is constantly evaluating and managing team members to identify the best players and maximize team results. Are you?

Recruiting - *Medi/Spa Coaching Model*
A medi/spa head coach must focus on the utilization of the starting team and the recruitment of new players. Refrain from giving your team members equal guest rotation. Identify the starters and assign more guests to them. This will increase the medi/spa's performance exponentially.

In the book *Topgrading*, Bradford Smart grades the players by A, B, C. The goal is to recruit A and B players and elevate the C players' performance. Do not prolong poor performance or C players if they are not the right fit for your team.

Identify your starting team through:
- Guest satisfaction rate
- Performance and skill
- Work ethic and professionalism
- Continuing education
- Attitude and teamwork

4. **Head Coach - *Sports Coaching Model***
In sports, the head coach is ultimately responsible for team performance. If the team is performing, the head coach is recognized. If the team is producing poor results, the head coach is usually terminated.

Prior to the start of the season, all players attend a pre-season boot camp. They go over plays, learn how to play as a team, run practice drills, and rehearse each play over and over. During this process, the coach is constantly seeking ways to improve their game. The team has a playbook for planning offensive and defensive strategies. After boot camp, they maintain a training schedule for the entire season.

The coach provides mental and physical workouts to stay fit and maximize performance in order to stay competitive. They never stop training.

During the game, where do you find the coach? On the sideline watching, supporting, motivating, strategizing... not in the office or in the locker room. They actively watch the team's performance.

The coach communicates to the team throughout the game. Coaches call a time-out when they need to refocus the team or change the team's game plan. They are continuously planning, strategizing, and making adjustments to win the game.

You may be thinking... professional sports players and coaches earn millions of dollars. That is true; however, everyone in the medi/spa industry can earn more if we apply the same coaching and training discipline to our organizations.

Head Coach - *Medi/Spa Coaching Model:*
The medi/spa head coach is responsible for the team's performance and skill. The coach's decisions influence the team's ability to win or lose the game. In order to stay in business and generate profits, the medi/spa head coach is responsible for the continuous improvement of the guest experience and for maximizing retail and service opportunities.

To be an effective medi/spa head coach, implement the following coaching model:

- Define head coach responsibilities
- Formulate a game plan and medi/spa curriculum

- Hold an annual Medi/Spa Boot Camp emphasizing coaching & training
- Establish a continuous training/coaching schedule
- Develop and analyze profit strategies
- Incorporate coaching observations into operation
- Utilize time-out coaching moments to focus the team
- Conduct head coach strategic planning meetings

5. **Performance Measures - *Sports Coaching Model***
   In professional sports, performance is everything. During every game, members of the organization track every statistic possible. They track points scored, blocks, steals, fumbles, turnovers, and much more. In addition to tracking statistics, players and coaches designate time to watch game tapes to evaluate effort and identify areas of improvement. After the coaching team reviews all statistics and game tapes, they adjust their team's strategy accordingly.

   Why all the focus on tracking statistics and measuring performance? Without tracking and identifying what is broken or weak, it is very hard, if not impossible, to make improvements.

   Performance Measures – Medi/*Spa Coaching Model*
   Track the team's performance on a daily basis. Establish daily, weekly, and monthly targets and goals. Compare actual performance vs. targets. Make adjustments to keep the team focused and aimed toward success.

   Below are Key Performance Indicators (KPI):
   - Volume per guest for service and retail
   - Guest retention rate
   - Upgrade service opportunities
   - Cross-team marketing
   - Training participation

- Guest experience, protocols, and rituals
- Attitude, attendance, and work ethic

6. **Team Recognition - *Sports Coaching Model***

    In sports, achievers are frequently recognized by their head coach. When a player is a superstar, they are asked to endorse products and services, invited to play in the all-star game, have personalized merchandise, etc. Being recognized for small or large accomplishments is a very valuable and necessary coaching function to maximize motivation and achievements.

    Team Recognition – Medi/*Spa Coaching Model*

    People today are looking for a lot more than a paycheck. They want to be valued and recognized! Implementing an awards program and recognizing the medi/spa team for their efforts and achievements is essential to the medi/spa's continuous success. Recognition provides the team with a sense of appreciation. It drives the team to excel and enhance their performance. In addition, the team's positive morale will elevate productivity and profits. Positively focused teams produce positive results!

    Focus on Coaching and Soar!

    The coaching profession is soaring! From personal and business coaching to executive and team coaching, professionals are elevating their knowledge and advancing organizations and careers through coaching.

    Coaching provides a fresh perspective on challenges and opportunities while enhancing performance and overall skill. Coaching helps build, retain, and strengthen teams. In both business and sports, coaching is a key ingredient to the success of the organization. If your organization is not achieving its goals, it is time to hire a professional coach.

The International Coaching Federation describes coaching as a partnership between a qualified coach and an individual or a team supporting the achievement of extraordinary results, based on goals set by the individual or the team. Through the coaching process, actions are focused to successfully produce relevant results.

Coaching provides:
- Clarity
- Focus
- Productive results
- Maximized potential
- Improved performance

A successful medi/spa needs a head coach! Who is your coach?

Dori Recommends….

To help you with your business you can reserve a CoachMe Private session.

Chapter 6:
Success Strategies

"There are no secrets to success. It is the result of preparation, hard work and learning from failures."
- Colin Powell

You Want to Open a Medi/Spa?

While I was at a recent show, I met few new medi/spa owners who have been in the business for one or two years. Unfortunately, they were having difficulties making ends meet and they were seeking our help to avoid closing their doors. This is extremely sad. Of course, they all envisioned building a beautiful and *successful* business. However, some essential planning steps to ensure long-term success and sustainability were not addressed.

Venturing into owning and operating a medi/spa is sometimes taken lightly. Many entrepreneurs feel that because they are successful business people in other fields or because they have an MBA, they can plan and operate their medi/spa without medi/spa industry experience, professional advice, or expert assistance.

A lot goes into planning and positioning a medi/spa for success. Here are eight myths and some valuable advice to help you save time and money.

Myth One: Build it and they will come.
Business Plan & Feasibility Study

Creating a detailed business plan and a feasibility study are the foundation of your medi/spa business venture. This is where you outline your vision, business strategies, type of medi/spa, positioning, and capital investment.

The feasibility study is the financial blueprint to your new venture. It outlines all financial aspects of your business. It should include initial investment by room, fixed cost, variable cost, a budget, revenue projections, return on your investment, surplus needed, and so on.

Myth Two: I can do it by myself.
Hiring a Medi/Spa Expert

Can you do it by yourself? Yes, but how successful will you be and how much time will it take you? You can work hard or you can work smart… Choosing the right medi/spa expert is crucial, especially during the pre-planning phase. Beware, there are many faux spa experts giving bad advice and collecting large sums of money. How should you select a medi/spa expert? Ask for references, work history, past projects, skills, area of expertise, and specialty. The right advisor will help you build a strong foundation for your business.

Myth Three: It looks like a good location….
Market Research – Location

You've heard it before: "Location, location, location!" Yes, it *is* everything when you're opening a day spa or a medical spa. It's essential to identify the target market as well as determine demographics and psychographics. In addition, you will also need to conduct a competitive analysis and forecast market share potential. Market research will also be useful when creating the medi/spa menu and selecting the type of services and medi/spa programs you will offer.

Myth Four: I have enough money.
Investment and Funding

Though you are excited and you have a positive outlook, account for opening delays, budget deficits, and high expenses. Plan for it, because something unexpected *usually* happens. You need to have deep pockets in case outside circumstances arise that you can't control, like a bad or slowing economy. Developing a medi/spa is costly. Make sure you account for all initial capital investments and all expenses to clearly define your financial picture.

Myth Five: We don't need to worry about the menu now.
Medi/Spa Concept, Guest Experience, and Menu

The guest experience or the medi/spa program should be one of the first things you do - not the last! Determining the experience is essential for space planning (pre-construction) and guest flow. It also helps determine the type of equipment and space you will need. The menu is critical to your medi/spa's identity and will help define the medi/spa's personality and image.

Myth Six: I only need an architect.
Planning the Medi/Spa Facility Space – Equipment, Furniture, Design

I have visited many beautiful medi/spas designed by some of the most renowned architects. But when it comes to functionality, several simply don't work. This is where a medi/spa consultant's input is very useful. They are able to work with your architect to ensure that the medi/spa is functional, beautiful, and profitable. It's not only about beauty; it's also about functionality. The back of the house is as important as the front, but in many medi/spas, the back of the house does not even exist!

Myth Seven: We'll do the marketing after we're up & running.
Marketing Plan

An annual marketing plan and marketing materials must be created a minimum of six months prior to opening date. Assigning the marketing duty to an expert could mean the difference between success and failure. Choose your marketing mix and develop a timeline to launch your marketing campaigns. Make sure your website is developed and running before your medi/spa is open for business.

Myth Eight: I'm not worried about finding the right team.
Recruiting and Hiring the Right Team

Hire the medi/spa director at least six months prior to opening. There are so many things to do in order to build the right team and to structure the organization properly. When choosing a medi/spa location, make sure the human capital pool is within reach. You don't want a small or limited amount of medi/spa professionals within the region. It makes selecting and hiring people difficult.

Mistakes to avoid:

1. **Retail space, an after-thought....** Create a medi/spa boutique. You could generate up to $500 per square foot in revenue from retail! Don't miss out on this income opportunity; plan for it.

2. **No team lounge....** You step into the medi/spa and see all the team members are "hanging out" by the front desk, here and there... because there is no team lounge.

3. **Product storage....** Not having appropriate storage for retail and professional products makes managing inventory complicated. Depending on the size of your medi/spa, having a product dispensary is a great way to control product costs.

4. **Overbuilding....** Often, we see this with resort spas. A resort may have 200 hotel rooms and build a 10- or 15-room spa without taking into account where the spa visitors will come from. As a result of overbuilding, the spa will operate at a

very low capacity and will not deliver the revenue forecast or expectations needed to be an independent profit center.

5. **Story....** Not developing a story or an identity will make it difficult to sell your products and services. Make sure you include it on your website and in your media kit.

6. **Medi/Spa images....** So many medi/spas do not include pictures of their medi/spa on their website or pictures of treatments. Remember, a picture is worth a thousand words.

7. **Training....** Don't think the only team training you need is technical training. If you want your medi/spa to succeed, you will need to teach the team how to promote your products and services.

8. **Compensation plan....** Don't follow what everyone else is paying. This is a big problem in the medi/spa industry. Look into innovative compensation plans, such as the "VPG ComPlan" from InSPAration Management. It's structured to pay the team their true worth based on volume per guest.

9. **Budget....** Not having a detailed budget will cripple you. You want to be able to manage your business, not have it manage you. A budget is a financial management tool to help chart your financial success. Don't have the time to create one? You may purchase one by visiting: www. InSPArationManagement.com

Dori Recommends....

To help you with your business you can tap into the following effective tools:

You are invited to join a business coach for a strategy session to help you define your vision and give you an overview of the medi/spa industry.

Email us at info@InSPArationManagement.com **with a request. Mention the book.**

Fall in Love with Your Business Again!

As a consulting firm, we hear from two different types of medi/spa owners:

1. The people who are frustrated, overwhelmed, or unhappy and are looking for ways to improve their business. It is sad but true that sometimes the call for help should have been made a lot earlier. These owners are reacting to their problems instead of planning for their success.

2. The people who are doing well, but who want to do better. These owners desire to take their business to the next level and map out a growth strategy. They are the people who really love their business! They are proactive about taking advantage of preventative care.

Your business is like your body: If you don't eat right, exercise, clean it, take care of it, etc., sooner or later you will end up at the doctor's office, or worse, in the ICU. Your business is the same. That is why it's important to love it and take great care of it so it can take care of you!

Entrepreneurs go into business to achieve the following goals:
A. Gain more freedom (to do whatever they love to do whenever they want).
B. Make more money (to live the lifestyle they feel they deserve).
C. Do what they love.

To be successful, you need a blueprint, a recipe to follow!
Look around you. Most successful businesses today are franchises. From Starbucks, to Massage Envy, and hundreds of other franchises, the main reason for their success is due

to systems, structure, and the blueprint they have for success.

At some point, someone loved their business enough to invest in it and to create that recipe for success. Do you love your business enough to gain a successful blueprint? Do you love it enough to invest in it so you can achieve the goals for having more freedom and make more money?

The point is if you love your business, you will invest in its success!

When we first launched InSPAration Management, I thought our clients would be the people who are really doing badly in business, but what we found was totally different.

Here are the facts:
1. The people who really need the business help rarely reach out for it. That is why so many businesses fail.
2. Most of our clients are the people who are already successful and want to be *more* successful.

This fact is proven to me over and over again when we host the Leap Ahead Medi/Spa Leader Seminar (https://www.insSPArationManagement.com/leap-ahead-spa-medi-spa-business-seminar/). Often, the people who attend generate seven figures in revenue, or they have smaller businesses but are generating six figures and wish to expand and invest in their growth. Which one are you? Do you seek help, or do you think you can do it on your own, always trying to reinvent the wheel?

Remember, one of the habits covered in *Seven Habits of Highly Effective People* by Stephen Covey is, "Sharpening the Saw!" Take the time now to sharpen your saw by attending the Leap Ahead Seminar, where you will gain your blueprint for success!

Six Steps to Enhance Your Medi/Spa Leadership

Shouldn't that be the most important thing? Without success, your leadership will quickly vanish. I encourage you to make a list of what is important to you as a leader and share that list with your team during your next team meeting. Ask your team what is most important and have them write their responses down on a board and/or post them in the team lounge. It's a great exercise to do to remind everyone why you do what you do.

1. What is One Problem You Can Turn into an Opportunity?

You've heard the saying, "When life gives you lemons, make lemonade." What lemons are in your medi/spa? How can you turn them into lemonade? Look at your problems as opportunities to enhance your skills. Problems make you stronger and allow you to grow. Don't push them under the rug and hope they go away because they won't. One question I am often asked is, "How do I motivate my team?" One of my answers is to engage your team in problem solving. This practice makes your team feel important and makes them aware that you value their input. It will motivate them and get them focused on positive results. They'll love being part of the solution!

2. What Does My Team Need to Hear From Me?

One of the most important leadership skills is communication. Ask yourself, what if you were a team member and you had a leader like yourself, what would you think of this leader? Sometimes the way we see ourselves is not the same as what others see. Look in the mirror. Examine what messages you are sending to the team. Are you a positive leader? How well do you communicate your vision to your team? Think from your employees' point of view — if they don't feel understood, they won't listen to you. Resist the urge to tell them how they "should" think or feel. Remember that inspiration comes from the heart!

3. As a Leader, Do You Know Your Clients' Greatest Needs?

When was the last time you did a survey to rediscover your guests' needs? Have you assessed your menu lately to see what treatments you need to stop offering and what new services you need to add to your menu? When was the last time you looked at guest comment cards? Get a focus group together and discover their pain or needs. Then offer solutions to address their specific concerns and watch your guest loyalty and success soar!

4. What New Business Relationships Should You Pursue?

The medi/spa industry is shifting from pampering to wellness. You can make this shift much easier by establishing new business-to-business relationships. Go out and meet people who can partner with you to provide wellness programs. Seek out acupuncturists, nutritionists or dietitians, life coaches, and other wellness professionals.... These are the types of relationships that you should focus on so you can reposition your medi/spa and build a new wellness business.

5. How Can You Be More Strategic?

See the big picture and get serious about setting the direction. Share the big picture with your team. Set aside time on your calendar for strategic planning. Conduct brainstorming sessions and chart a path. You can't expect things to get better on their own. You have to have a road map, navigate your way, and lead the driving force to change.

6. What Leadership Skill Can You Improve?

Improve your leadership skills by building your success library. Do you have one? Invest in sharpening your skills and experience exponential growth!

The Art of Medi/Spa Merchandising

Is your boutique piquing your guests' interest and generating a profit? If you answered no, it's time to assess your boutique's effectiveness. Calculate your profit per square foot and your volume per guest. A profitable boutique takes planning, managing, and tracking. The following seven steps will help you create an attractive and profitable boutique!

1. Inventory Management
Check your merchandising mix performance. Run reports to identify your product mix performance. This report should be generated by product, by brand, and by type to identify your best, medium, and low sellers. Then identify the most and least popular price point to determine how much your guests are willing to spend on products and merchandise. Who within your medi/spa is responsible for inventory management and boutique performance? Identify that person and outline their responsibilities.

2. Selecting Your Merchandising Mix
Your merchandising mix should include items other than skincare, hair, and nail products. Your mix should include items to continue the medi/spa experience at home and other fun and unique items that guests won't find in a typical retail outlet. Product mix suggestion: If you use it during the experience, you should sell it!

Relaxation Lounge
Many medi/spas offer some type of food and beverage within the relaxation area. Include items such as tea, dried

fruits, energy bars, etc. It's wise to sell the items you offer. When people like things they try, they will buy them. Use shelf talkers to explain the benefits of each item you offer your guests. Sell the tea they drink, sell the energy bars, and sell the mixed nuts or dried fruits.

Rituals
When you use essential oil as a ritual in the treatment room, sell the oils in the boutique.

Mood Enhancements
When you burn candles, sell the candles.

Changing Lounge
If you have showers in the changing lounge, use the shampoo, conditioner, shower gel, and moisturizer that you sell within the facilities. Many medi/spas make the mistake of using inexpensive products in the showers and then selling a different product in the boutique. That is a big disconnect. It might cost you a little more to have the more expensive products in the showers, but in the long run, you will sell a lot more products.

3. The Art of Merchandising
When you display products, attempt to tell a story. Show the professional treatment and the home care that goes with it. Do the same for body products.

Use props such as bowls, cups, trays, frames, accessories, etc. to add interest to the shelf.

Identify products' natural ingredients and purchase them at local grocery stores, florists, etc. Incorporating these natural ingredients and elements will add unique ambiance and great character to your display area. Items such as leaves, botanicals, apples, pears, oranges, chamomile, lavender, herbs, etc. will add interest to the merchandise.

Reserve one shelf for your promotion or monthly special. Don't overcrowd shelves. Practice "less is more." Rotating your merchandise is essential. It gives the impression that you have new items even when you don't.

Testers are essential to selling products. Most people like to touch, smell, and feel products. Make sure you give them the opportunity. Department stores generate substantial amounts of sales with the sampling model. You can, too!

4. Point of Purchase Items
Place irresistible items near the check-out area so guests can grab and add to their ticket. POP items need to be $20 or less.

5. Discovery Station
Placing a discovery station in either the relaxation lounge or in your boutique area provides you with opportunity to introduce particular items to your guests. Allow them to discover and learn about a particular product and treatment. Change it biweekly or monthly.

6. Revenue Generation
How much revenue are you generating from your boutique?

Retail Revenue Calculation:
By Square Foot
Total Retail Revenue / Total Boutique Square Footage = Retail Revenue per Square Foot
By Volume per Guest
Total Retail Revenue / Total Number of Guests to the Medi/Spa = Retail Volume per Guest (RVPG)

7. Setting Your Boutique Goals

Decide how much volume you would like to generate from your medi/spa boutique and expand upon the above six steps.

Mistakes to Avoid:

- Products behind locked doors
- No medi/spa boutique or limited retail area
- No product display or visuals in treatment rooms
- No pre-packaged items, POP, or to-go promotions
- Unorganized, too much clutter, or not enough products
- Not managing your inventory properly

Should you need additional information or assistance in improving your merchandising within your medi/spa, contact a medi/spa business solutions firm for assistance.

Chapter 7:

Medi/Spa BizTools

"Profit in business comes from repeat customers, customers that boast about your service, and that bring friends with them."
- W. Edwards Deming

What is the Best Way to Set Team Goals?

Setting goals is a very important business and personal tool. Unfortunately, many medi/spas do not practice it on regular basis. As a matter of fact, a Harvard University study published that only 3% of the American population sets goals in writing. Napoleon Hill, the author of the bestselling book *Think and Grow Rich* says, "A person without a goal is like a ship without a rudder."

As a medi/spa leader, you need to set the overall goals for your medi/spa. Set monthly volume goals for:
- Service volume
- Retail volume
- Other programs

Divide the overall goals by department. Then divide each department's goal by the number of team members within that department. Now each person has their own goal/target to achieve.

At the beginning of each month, the medi/spa leader should pass out department and individual targets to each person, and at the end of the month, measure these targets against the team's actual performance.

The following is the SMART method of setting goals:
Specific: Goals must be **clear** and **specific.**
Measurable: **Track, evaluate** and **measure** your progress.
Attainable: Not too **high**, not too **low.**
Relevant: **Relevant** to the grand scheme of the goal.
Time-bound: Have a **starting** and an **ending** point.

If some of your team members are not achieving their goals, take the time to train and coach them in order to improve performance.

Nine Common Mistakes for Time Utilization

Do you often feel overwhelmed, or as if you are spinning your wheels, or you can never finish all the things you need to do? Or maybe your days seem to go from one crisis to another, putting out fires. If you answered yes, that may be a sign of poor time utilization. Let's face it, we could all use help to better manage our time.

We all have good intentions. We want to be more productive and complete our tasks, and there is no better feeling than achieving our goals. Being productive helps us be happier, more positive, relaxed, and obtain balance in our lives.

In this section, you'll discover nine of the most common mistakes people make in using their time.

Mistake #1: No To Do List
Is your day full of obligations and you are running around from one thing to another causing you to forget to do something important? If so, that's probably because you don't have a to do list.

Having a to do list is a great way to stay on track. Use an A - C coding system (A for high priority items, C for very low priorities). Nightly, you should have your list ready for the next day. When you create your list, make sure you differentiate between a project list and a to do list.

For example, if you are going to work on a strategic plan, such as a medi/spa budget, marketing plan, etc., set aside enough time each day so it won't cause you to procrastinate or miss key steps. It would be wise to break large tasks or projects down into specific, actionable steps. Then, you won't overlook something important.

Mistake #2: No Goals

Do you know where you'd like to be in six months? What about this time next year, or even five years from now? If not, it's time to set some goals!

It's wise to set three types of goals: personal, business, and spiritual. You should also set short-term and long-term goals. Goal setting is essential because it helps you manage how you spend your time. When you know where you want to go, you can manage your priorities, time, and resources to get there. Goals also help you decide what's worth spending your time on and what's a distraction.

Mistake #3: Not Prioritizing

Once you create your to do list, you must prioritize it. This allows you to manage your tasks and keeps you on track. Some urgent task may come up from time to time and you need to tend to it. Once you take care of this urgent matter, you must get back to your to do list. Make sure you prioritize your list.

Mistake #4: Managing Distractions and Interruptions

Are you practicing the "open door" policy? Don't! Distractions and interruptions can kill productivity and working on your to do list. Close your door and be productive.

Did you know that you could lose as much as two hours a day to distractions? Interruptions may come from emails, medi/spa team members, colleagues in a crisis, clients, or phone calls; they all prevent us from achieving our goals. If you want to gain control of your day, don't allow distractions and interruptions to get in the way.

Mistake #5: Procrastination

Procrastination is when you put off tasks until later that you should be focusing on right now. Sometimes we have busy work instead of productive work. We use that as an excuse to procrastinate on something that we need to do. If you have to do something, just do it. Procrastinating will weigh heavy on you.

Placing a timeline on projects and things that you must do will help you manage procrastination. Don't let procrastination get the best of you. The results will make you feel overwhelmed and anxious. Instead, focus on devoting a small amount of time to starting. That's all!

Mistake #6: Saying Yes Too Often

Do you have a hard time saying no? Saying no to certain things is ok! Don't feel obligated to take on too much. You can't be everything to everybody. You need to keep your schedule in mind and if you can't do something, simply say, "No, I can't at this time." It's better to say no now than to say yes and disappoint them later. The other thing to keep in mind is the ability to delegate and avoid micro-managing. This will free you to maybe say yes to something you would *like* to do.

Mistake #7: The Juggler - Multi-Tasking

How many balls do you have up in the air? Don't think that you can be Superman or Superwoman. Sooner or later, the balls are going to start dropping. Multi-tasking is good some of the time, but not all the time. You can accomplish things faster and more accurately if you focus on one thing at a time. You will save more time and avoid mistakes that result in re-doing tasks.

Mistake #8: Not Coming Up For Air

It's nice to think that you can work non-stop, but that may not be the best thing for you (I need to practice this). It's important to take breaks and come up for air. You will be able to think much more clearly when you take a mental break. Your brain will be able to recharge. It's good to take a mini mental vacation by using a breathing exercise with some essential oils to help you re-energize and then you can go back to work. Thomas Edison used to take a power nap all the time while working on his inventions. If you can't take a power nap, you can always take a few minutes to meditate.

Mistake #9: Bad Schedule

We all have our favorite time to work when we are most productive. Some of us are morning people and some are night owls. When is your most productive time? Know that and take care of the most important tasks during that time. Think of your high-energy time and schedule accordingly.

Special tip: We all have the same amount of time.
- 7 days per week x 24 hours = 168 hours per week.
- Take out 40 hours for work.
- 50 hours for sleep.
- You will have 72 hours left.
- Deduct 3 hours per day getting ready and travel.
- That will leave you with 51 hours of spare time.

If you invest two hours per day back into yourself and your medi/spa business (that is 14 hours per week), you will have 37 hours left. That is an average of more than five hours per day of free time. The two hours you will invest in improving yourself and your business will move you from average to superior. Tap into business solutions and watch your medi/spa grow!

Dori Recommends….

To help you with your business you can tap into the following effective tools:

Recipes For Success

Secrets to Avoid Sabotaging Your Success

As entrepreneurs, we are expected to lead the way and be on 24/7. Sometimes, owning a business comes with massive pressure, frustration, and headaches. In most cases, we bring stress onto ourselves by not properly structuring our business. We know this is true because we talk to medi/spa leaders every day and we work together to resolve these issues. You can't be successful by yourself. It takes a team, but not just any team. The team needs to be carefully selected. Here are five big mistakes entrepreneurs make when building and managing their teams.

1. No Position Description
One of the biggest frustrations of having a business is managing the team. Are you running a business or a babysitting service? 90% of your frustration can disappear if you take the time to interview and select properly. A well-thought out, detailed position description and expectations list will dramatically reduce stress and frustration. With this structure in place, you will have more time to focus on your business and minimize time spent on managing people. Imagine how much more productive your business will be when the entire team knows exactly what is expected of them.

2. Not Enough Delegation
The philosophy of, "No one can do it as good as I can," needs to disappear. That's a sign of weakness and poor leadership. You must be able to delegate; you can't do everything yourself. However, you need to invest the time and money in training the person(s) you will be delegating to. The secret to successful delegation is detailed instruction and clearly outlined expectation of results.

3. Too Much Autonomy

The definition of autonomy is, "The quality or state of being independent, free, and self-directed." Autonomy is an issue we frequently encounter in the medi/spa industry. Autonomy is good if the team member is an A player. In many cases, medi/spas are managed with too much autonomy to undeserving team members. Giving too much autonomy usually indicates the inability to track work progress, to identify potential problems, or to evaluate team member performance. Sometimes, you get blindsided by problems that are costly and aggravating. It's a better practice to take a few minutes every week and evaluate. This will help you stay on track to ensure your success.

4. Quick to Hire, Slow to Fire!

The problem is sometimes you get in a bind and you hire just to hire. You hire fast just to get the job off your hands... but when you get the wrong person on your team, it ends up costing you a fortune!

When Jack Welch was the CEO of GE, he practiced cutting the bottom 10% from his organization. So if you do end up hiring the wrong person, don't hang on to them. Continually monitor your bottom 10% and replace them until you have a super team. You don't want a sinking ship.

5. Re-Creating the Wheel

This is a biggie... we see this too often. You don't need to be re-creating the wheel over and over. You need to have proven and effective structure, systems, and training manuals. Once they are created, your job is much easier.

How many times have you found yourself answering the same questions over and over again? Do you constantly search for your shortcut notes on scraps of paper or post its? Anytime you find yourself doing or saying the same thing twice, it's time to create a template. That way, the next time the same situation comes up, everyone knows what to do. You have more important things to do... like marketing your business and generating revenue!

"Everything is a system. The purpose of a system is to free you to do the things you want to do." Quoted from one of my favorite books for business owners, *The E-Myth Revisited* by Michael E. Gerber.

Detoxify Your Business and Plan for Financial Health!

Toxins are deadly, not only to our bodies but also to our business. When was the last time you gave your business a good check-up and detoxification? Been a while? *Now* is the perfect time to do it! As the years go by, we always hope and pray that the New Year is going to be better than the previous. But the only way that becomes reality is if we make changes and improvements. There is a saying: "What got you here won't get you there!" To gain new results, you need new action! You need to detoxify and implement healthy habits. It's time to practice what you preach to your clients!

The Business Detoxification Plan

1. **Financial Detoxification**
   What is keeping you from having a healthy business? Run your annual financial reports:
   - Balance Sheet
   - P&L Statement
   - Cash Flow
   - Calculate your Financial Ratios
   - Overall Revenue
   - Operating Expenses
   - Compensation
   - Profits

Would you give your business performance an A, B, or C? Hopefully not a failing grade!

Most important is that you made a profit and you paid yourself. Did you? Discover what is making money and what is not. Purge what is not.

Strong Financial Health Strategies: Two Quick Ways to Boost Your Revenue

Focus on Building Your Membership Business
Do you have a Membership Program? If yes, I am sure you can have your guest relations team promote it more and sign more people up. If you don't have a membership program, get your hands on the *Ten Steps to Creating and Launching your Membership Program* USB and learn how to implement it! Memberships are a great way to increase retention rate and revenue.

Get Serious About Retail Sales Opportunities
To improve medi/spa retail sales, I encourage you to implement The PRIDE System from the *Don't Sell, Recommend!* USB. Set some consequences to enforce and watch your sales soar! You can do it!

2. **Organizational Structure – The Five W's**
   Who, What, Where, When, Why. Is it clear to everyone what you are trying to accomplish and how you are going to get there? Or is everyone singing from their own hymn book? It's time to let go of toxic team members. If they don't want to sing your song, they need to join another group. Enough is enough!

   Healthy Organizational Strategy
   Publish defined position descriptions, employee manuals, expectations, policies, procedures, systems, etc. Clarify who is who. Tap into the nine medi/spa business manuals we have to help you get healthy by the book!

3. **"You've Got to be Kidding Me" Guest Experience**
   Your guest experience is a direct reflection of your retention rate. If you have a high retention rate, this indicates that your team and your guest experiences are great. If you have

a low retention rate, you not only have toxins but cancer as well. You need emergency work and intensive care! How good is your retention rate?

Healthy Retention Rate

The easiest way to increase retention is by delivering a great and consistent guest experience. You need to have a skilled team, engage your clients, build relationships, stay in touch, and get feedback…. Implement healthy habits and you will have lifetime clients and sales will soar!

4. **Toxic Team**

   Your team can make you or break you. Some leaders always have an excuse for bad performance. There is only one reason for bad performance: not being prepared. It's just like when you are in school and have a test. If you didn't study and don't do your homework, you are going to fail. Stop the excuses. Take a good look at your team and your leadership skills. Are they good students or failing?

   ## Healthy Team

   Recruit and hire the *right* way from the beginning! Implement The CLARITI Hiring System and build a strong team. Set expectations from the very beginning. Make them sign a commitment agreement and outline your standards. Let them know you are serious about success. If you already have a team, you may want to have everyone re-interview or have a fresh start meeting. Call us, we can help! Set a new healthy path for your entire team!

New Success

Have you assessed your business lately? Now is the time to analyze your results. Take a good look at how you've been doing things and decide what you need to do differently. You know the saying, "If you keep doing what you've always done, you will keep getting the same results." Don't keep doing the same things you did; expect greater results! It's time to do things differently. It's time for a new business model. It's time to reposition your medi/spa and tap into new revenue streams. It's time to make *profit!*

New Business Model: Excerpts from the Leap Ahead Medi/Spa Director Seminar

Are you still saying "indulge" or "pamper" in your marketing? Are you still offering the same treatments everyone else is offering? If you are, stop. *New model example:* Offer de-stress programs lasting three or four weeks instead of a one hour massage. Watch your revenue grow!

Are you still paying your team 40% or 50% commission or any kind of compensation that is not based on performance? If you are, stop. *New model example:* Set team expectations and tie compensation to performance. Begin measuring: volume per guest, retention rate, referral rate, and guest satisfaction, and see your profits leap!

Are you still operating your medi/spa without a budget? Do you know your financial ratios, such as your overall product cost, compensation cost, expenses, and profit margins? Do you know how many people should come to the medi/spa and how much each person should spend in your medi/spa? If you don't know or don't have a budget, it's time for change! *New model example:* Create a budget and financial structure. Identify new revenue streams to increase your revenue and build a sustainable business.

Are you still waiting for people to find you? Are you operating at a lower capacity than your true potential? Do you have a marketing plan? Is your plan well-defined or tested? Time to Improve! *New model example:* Plan annual marketing strategies that include several economical marketing mixes. Add automated communication to strengthen relationships and promote your products and services.

Are you still accepting that your team isn't selling retail products? This is causing you to lose a ton of money each year. *New model example:* Shift your team's philosophy regarding retail. It's not about what you *sell*; it's about *what your medi/spa does for your clients*. Why are you in the medi/spa business? To help people! Are you helping people by letting them leave without proper recommendations?

New Results
I am sure you are ready for new results; but as mentioned, to achieve greater profits you need new actions. Designate some time for strategic planning to elevate your success.

Five Strategies to Spring into Action!

Spring is the time of year to clean house. It's a good time to take a look at what you have done so far for the year and make necessary adjustments. If you delay this process, before you know it another year will pass by without springing forward.

1. **Get Organized**

   You may be familiar with the Perato Principle, also known as the 80/20 rule. It states that 80% of your results come from only 20% of your actions, which means that people are busy, but they are not always being productive. There is a big difference between the two. Being productive is about planning the day, being organized, and accomplishing goals. Chaos and disorganization have a big price. I encourage you to schedule time to get organized this month so you can be more productive. Don't let disorganization hold you back, block your success, and add stress to your life.

2. **Plan Your Marketing**

   Marketing is the heartbeat of your business! Without marketing, your business will be stale and cripple growth. If you want to spring into action, you need to plan your medi/spa marketing. Create exciting medi/spa promotions, plan the appropriate marketing material, and launch them properly. Get your team involved in the planning process! Set sales goals, train everyone on what they need to say to promote them, and increase revenue! If you need help with a medi/spa marketing plan, check out the new www.CoachMeOnDemand.com site we just launched. It allows you to tap into the Marketing for Success CoachMe Gold tele-seminars.

3. **Host a Medi/Spa Spring Event**

   Events are a great way to generate buzz, excitement, and revenue for your medi/spa. You should have one event a quarter, and spring is a great time for one! Come up with a great theme, plan the activities, giveaways, demonstrations, specials, refreshments, your medi/spa dollars, and so on... an event can generate major amounts of revenue if it is planned properly! Go back and listen to the *Success with Event Planning* USB and make sure you implement all the strategies into your plan.

4. **Set Time Aside For Training**

   People ask me all the time what makes one medi/spa succeed and another fail. My answer is the focus on medi/spa business training. Medi/Spa leaders who schedule time for team training are the ones who are experiencing exponential growth. Medi/Spa leaders who belong to the CoachMe Gold series provide their medi/spa with monthly coaching to keep improving. Everyone needs a coach, a mentor to reach a high level of success! Yes, it takes an investment, but this investment is one you can't afford *not* to make. Schedule time to train your team on medi/spa business and watch your performance soar!

5. **Stay Motivated**

   Last week I received a phone call from a doctor who owns a medi-spa. She sounded so unmotivated and down. By the time she got off the phone, she was excited and motivated again! As a leader you can't afford to be unmotivated. If you are unmotivated, your team will be as well. Motivation and excitement are contagious. You need to stay on top of your game. Remember your purpose and why you are doing what you are doing. But if you feel unmotivated, call me to help you get back on track. Private Medi/Spa Executive Coaching is a great way to have someone there for you and hold you accountable!

Dori Recommends….

To help you with your business you can tap into the following effective tools:

Genius Marketing and Sales Strategies

A GPS for Your Medi/Spa Business

Directions, maps, blueprints, and plans are all essential steps for any journey. Maybe you are currently planning your summer vacation; you may fly, or you may choose to take a long road trip. The one thing that I know you will do for sure is map out your journey. You will decide the when, where, who, and why of your trip. You may use your GPS to guide you or you may stop by your AAA location for a map. Either way, you will have a guide for your trip so you don't get lost on your journey, right?

As a business owner, you take a journey daily. What do you use to chart your daily success? Do you have a GPS for your business? Or are you just praying you will reach your desired destination by chance?

Everyone needs a GPS to have a successful business, and you are in luck, because InSPAration Management specializes in it. Here are four essential tips to help you reach your destination safely and successfully.

1. **Know where you want to go and who is going with you!**
   You may already have a medi/spa business, or maybe you are thinking about taking the plunge. Either way, you need a plan. Your plan starts with a vision. We have all heard that we have to have a vision of what we want our businesses to look like.

   How clear is your vision? Do you know where you want to take your business and who will go with you? You see, just like the GPS, you can put in the address and it will take you to your desired destination. The plan, or your business GPS, should work the same way. If you have a plan for your success, you are more likely to be successful. But if you are going to work every day and just wander around, you feel like you are going somewhere when in all reality you are just going in circles. No one wants to go around in circles; we all want to reach a destination.

2. **Buy your business GPS to give you direction!**
The main recipe for a successful business is having direction. It's what I call the four SSSS's: Systems, Structure, Strategies and Solutions.

When you focus on the four SSSS's, you will have a successful medi/spa business. Some people try to create their own map or develop their own GPS, but why would you do that if someone already has the formula? Stop reinventing the wheel! There are many tools that you can tap into that will direct you to your destination faster and more effectively. Check out the new medi/spa manuals on our website for your medi/spa business GPS and gain a clear and successful map!

3. **Follow the GPS's directions.**
You can have the best GPS in the world, but if you don't listen and you don't follow directions, you will be lost or take a longer way to your destination. You can obtain your own business blueprint in several different ways:

    A.   Attend the Leap Ahead seminar
    B.   Own the Success Library
    C.   Join the CoachMe Gold Program
    D.   Own the Medi/Spa Manuals
    E.   Participate in Private Coaching

Yes, gaining direction requires an investment, but what is the alternative? Did you know that, according to the Department of Commerce, one million businesses open every year? But only 200,000 survive the first five years!

That means 800,000 fail. Why? They did not have good direction, the four SSSS's, or a good GPS.

4. **Keep updating your GPS.**
   Things are always changing, and unless we change with them, we will be left behind. Updating your GPS is very important so you can avoid taking the wrong turns as new roads open up. Consumers demand changes: new treatments are introduced, more innovative equipment is designed, and so on. If you don't innovate and keep updating, you will lose market share.

   Many medi/spa professionals have the InSPAration Management Business GPS, and we invite you to have it, too. We are so confident that it will help you that *we guarantee your satisfaction or your money back.*

   Do you want to ensure a successful journey? We encourage you to implement, be disciplined, be persistent, participate in medi/spa business training, and you will get there! Just like when you prepare for a trip, you don't expect to get where you want to go for free. You need to pay the price.

   Everything in life has a price, and it's the same for your business. If you want your business to be successful, you need to keep investing in it. You need a coach, just like any sports team has a coach. They don't just hire the team and say good luck. They invest in them and help them grow so they can develop into a championship team. Your business is the same. Invest in business education and you will experience exponential growth!

   "Finding Dori and InSPAration Management has been such an amazing experience! We started with Leap Ahead, then joined the CoachMe membership, which has been like having our own private coach all year round. Now, InSPAration

Management does all of our newsletters for us! The support, training, and guidance that we've received has taken my business from 'doing pretty good' to, 'Wow, I never imagined this kind of revenue was possible!' Implementing all of Dori's business management tools has been so extremely time saving and helpful for our entire management team. Just to name one, the Spa Business Manuals; I can only imagine how many hours it would have taken me to create manuals for each department. But all we had to do was make few edits to customize the manuals that InSPAration Management provided and now we have professional, impressive, and practical manuals for the entire spa team! Training is a pleasure now!

"Thanks to all of the training and encouragement I've received, my leadership and management skills have improved tremendously and my spa team now has direction, goals, and motivation! I enjoy my business now. Thank you, Dori!"

Jackie Martin
Jacqueline Morgan Day Spa

Get your Medi Spa and Spa Manuals now and gain the blueprint for success!

10 Important Reminders to Help You Succeed!

1. **Set Your Goals.** Napoleon Hill, the author of one of my favorite books, *Think and Grow Rich,* said, "A person without a goal is like a ship without a rudder." You don't want to live without defined goals. Write out short- and long-term goals for your business and your personal life. Clarify your goals as much as possible. Then, create an action plan for each goal. Prioritize and start mapping out every goal by creating a list of things that you need to do so you can begin taking action immediately!

2. **Enroll in a Coaching Program.** Everyone needs a coach. Without a coach, you are not going to win a championship. You can belong to one of the CoachMe programs we offer so your business will grow and flourish. One of the best things about having a coach is the accountability they provide.

3. **Get a Mentor.** When you talk with any successful entrepreneur, ask them how they became so successful. Most will tell you they had a great mentor. Whether this is a person you have to pay to speak with or someone who is willing to mentor you pro-bono, either way you should have a mentor.

4. **Read Books & Articles and Listen to Business CDs.** Continuing education will help you stay on the successful path. Turn your car into a university and listen to coaching CDs or USBs. Schedule some time each day to read rich business content. Sometimes all you need is one idea to grow into greater success.

5. **Improve Your Time Management and Productivity.** Many people don't stay focused and don't plan their daily tasks. If you want to be successful, you have to identify your daily

tasks and stick to a schedule. Don't get trapped in unproductive work. Make a commitment to do at least one thing every day to help your business grow!

6. **Wake Up Earlier.** Get motivated and start early. Interruptions are a terrible thing, making you lose focus and delaying progress. When you wake up early, you can accomplish your most important tasks first thing in the morning. This practice will help you be more productive.

7. **Plan Your Bucket List - Create a Vision Board.** Why are you working so hard? I was at a seminar in Chicago last month and the instructor asked the group, "What is your dream? Why are you working? What do you want?" Create your bucket list and put it on a vision board. Once you commit to it, you will be amazed how things will begin to turn into reality.

8. **Chart a Timeline for What You Want to Accomplish.** A dream or a wish list is just that unless you create an action plan with a timeline. This will help you stay on track. Use a calendar and schedule all your medi/spa business activities. You will be more likely to do what is on your schedule. Just like your medi/spa clients, make appointments. You need to make appointments for things you want to accomplish and stick to them!

9. **Script the Outcome in Advance.** Create a medi/spa success business journal to list your daily activity before the day starts. Script out all the outcomes you would like to have. It is amazing what will happen when you detail the outcome. Script your outcome for the day, the week, the month, and the year. Continue scripting on regular basis. Focus on *all* positive outcomes as if they already took place!

10. **Adopt a "Can Do" Mindset.** Negativity kills your goals and your dreams. When you have a "can do" attitude and mindset, you can move mountains! Don't let anyone rain on your parade or give you negative vibes. Walk away and choose to be part of a positive group who wants to succeed and move ahead in life. Choose your business peers and social contacts carefully. Be around people who are more successful than you! This will keep you motivated and you will learn from them.

Success is not rocket science; it is very simple. What you do need is a success recipe and an implementation plan. We can help you with both! Don't try to reinvent the wheel. This year, tap into medi/spa business tools that are proven effective and you will be well on your way. Need help? Sign up for a private CoachMe session. We can help you plan your success!

Chapter 8:
What's Next?
Assessment and Strategic Planning Time!

"The majority of people meet with failure because of their lack of persistence in creating new plans to take the place of those which fail."
- Napoleon Hill

How Healthy and Profitable is Your Business?

Just like with our bodies, we need to visit the doctor for an annual check-up, we need to do the same for our business to ensure growth and good financial health.

When was the last time your business had a check-up? Isn't it time for a professional assessment?

InSPAration Management can provide you with an onsite or remote assessment. To help you identify your strengths and challenges, we invite you to take all or one of the assessments on InSPArationManagement.com; the results are emailed to you immediately. You can assess the following segments of your business:

Financial
Identify your ratios

Marketing
New client acquisition and conversion rate

Website
Revenue and client engagement

Menu
Copy and image

Operational
Systems and structure

Team Compensation
Compensation model and performance

Secret Shopper
Guest experience and retention

To get you started, we invite you to take the online assessments and then reserve a strategic session with an InSPAration Management coach. **This is a complimentary session with your book purchase.**

Chapter 9:

Medi/Spa Resources

Accounting Software
Peachtree
QuickBooks

Authority Marketing
Become Published

Blogs/Branding/Marketing – InSPAration Management
InSPAration Management
Menu
Marketing Material
InSPAration Management BizTools – Marketing Plan &Webinars
Menu Done For Me Spa Marketing
Logon Event Material

Business Education/Consulting/Coaching
InSPAration Management-Executive Coaching-Mastermind Group
InSPAration Management-Business Webinars InSPAration
Management-Private On-site Training, Assessments,
Merchandising, Etc.
CoachMe Series Soaring Ahead
InSPArationManagement .com

Client Relation Management (CRM)
Infusionsoft

Clip Art & Stock Photos
ClipArt.com
iStock
ShutterStock

Collateral Material Design
InSPAration Management – Menu, Ads, Promotions, Brochures, E-
Marketing, Direct Mail, Corporate Image, Logo, Websites, etc.

Conferences
International Esthetics, Cosmetics & Spa Conference
ESI
Premier

A4M
American Med Spa Association
The Aesthetic Show

Conference Calls
No Cost Conference
Consumer E-zine Publishing Tool
Done For Me Spa Marketing!

Direct Mailing Lists
Info USA
SRDS

Domain Registration & Website Design
GoDaddy.com

E-mail Marketing Solutions
Constant Contact
iContact
Mail Chimp

E-Newsletter
InSPAration Moments - Your e-News Business Partner

Face & Body, Products, Makeup
Pevonia
NeoStrata
Jane Iredale
SkinCeuticals
Glo Minerals
Image Skin Co
Skin Medica
Zo
Obagi
Eminence
Mlis
PCA (peels)
Bella Lucce
Whish

Soaptopia
Farm House Fresh
Pure Fiji
Bubblina
Damone Roberts
Instantly Ageless
Eviron
Medicalia Skin Care
Isola
Moon Valley Organics
Aromandina Essential Oils
High Chi Energy Jewelry
Biofreeze

Finance
InSPAration Management BizTools- Medi/Spa Budget,
Compensation Plan, Financial Calculators, etc.

Gift Items
Body Brushes
Robes w/spa logo
Neck wraps
Loofas
Clarisonic
Jewelry –Sweet Romance
Ann Vaughn
Mud Pie
Aromatherapy
Poopourri
Water bottles w/spa logo
Tiger Tail- Massage items
Pino - Lotions, candles
Hair ties- Emi-Jay
Hanky Panky – lingerie
Epicuren
Theracane
Pendergrass
Accuball
Kashwere-plush robes

Sonoma Lavender
Simply - Clothes
Plant Life
Soy delicious
Jane

Hair
Redken, Pureology, Morracan Oil, Aveda, Mastey

Password
Lastpass

Postcards
Instant Telesminar

Printing Services
Docucopies
Overnight Prints
Vista Print

Retail Packaging
Green Groovy Bags
Howard Packaging
Max Pack, Nashville Wraps

Retail Products
Amrit Organic / Red Cherry Group
Aromandina
Candle Impressions
Comphy Linens
Derma Start
Flex Flop
Herbasway Spa and Beauty
Hay House Publishing
Cara Cosmetics
Definitions
Oka B
PooPourri

Pre de Provence
Spa Music
Sparkle Plenty
Sprayology
Tea Tassi
White Lion
Yeah Baby

Retail Merchandising Shelving
Smart Furniture

Secret Shopper
InSPAration Management

Social Media
InSPAration Management – Done For Me Marketing Facebook
LinkedIn
Twitter
You Tube
Facebook
Instagram

Software/POS
SpaWare – MD Ware
Millenium (Harms)
Mindbodyonline.com

Medi/Spa Equipment & General Supplies
Silhoutte Tone
Universal Companies
Lasers- Quanta, Cynosure, Alma
Medical – AmSpa Association, DaySpa Association

Trade Magazines & Websites
American Spa Magazine
Pulse Magazine
Skin Inc. Magazine

Uniforms
Spa Uniforms
Yeah Baby

Webinar
Zoom

About the Author

As a leading business advisor, Dori contributes to the success of medi spas and spas worldwide using the four S's. She applies them in her business, InSPAration Management, and in all her clients' business. She says, "Implementing the 4 S's will equal SUCCESS."

Dori began her professional career in the hospitality industry. She spent 18 years working her way up the corporate ladder with her last position as Vice President for the Wyndham Resorts. Once she hit the glass ceiling, Dori decided to go out on her own and start her own business development firm. This led her to work with skin care companies and the spa industry.

For the past 2 decades, Dori has focused all her time and efforts on developing effective business models for medi/spas.

Her efforts have contributed to the success of companies worldwide. Dori's clients are physicians, entrepreneurs, and business owners who are looking for a solid, proven effective business model to help them open, manage and profit with their medi/spas.

Dori's passion and strength is applying the 4S's – **Systems, Structure, Strategies, and Solutions** that are easy to implement, provide a great foundation for a medi spa or spa business, and equal SUCCESS.

When you see and hear Dori speak, you become a lifer. Her energetic delivery style is captivating and concise. She holds your attention with her expertise, enthusiasm, and sense of humor. 1000's of professionals have graduated from her business seminars.

Dori helps professionals **become published authors** with the Write Your Book In One Weekend seminar, improve their leadership skills with the Leap Ahead seminar and become millionaires by implementing the Millionaires' Circle.

Dori's best selling books **Spa Business Secrets to Increase Profit and 21 Strategies to Increase Profits are found on Amazon** and on many medi/spa professionals' desks. Her success library is filled with the most innovative ways to market, position, train, and build a high- performance team while experiencing exponential growth and sustainable business success.

Her business tools include Manuals, Podcasts, Webinars, Audios, and Videos.

Dori's most popular program is her CoachMe Mastermind group. This high-level coaching program is ideal for top-level medi/spa business professionals.

If you are looking to open, turn around or improve your current medi/spa, we invite you to learn more about Dori, all her programs and business tools by visiting www.InSPArationManagement.com

Dori lives in Orlando and Daytona Beach where her office is located. Her son Charlie is studying BioChemistry in Melbourne, Australia. Dori loves to travel. She has made friends in over 30 countries and 50 states. She also enjoys golfing, shopping, great wine and food!